BEST W

C000088569

[signature]

ERINDIPITY

The Irish Miscellany

DAVID KENNY

**MENTOR
BOOKS**

This Edition first published 2006 by

Mentor Books, 43 Furze Road, Sandyford Industrial Estate
Dublin 18

Tel. +353(0)1-295 2112/3   Fax. +353(0)1-295 2114
email: admin@mentorbooks.ie
www.mentorbooks.ie

ISBN-10: 1-84210-375-X
ISBN-13: 978-1-84210-375-3

A catalogue record for this book is available
from the British Library

Cover Illustration: Graham Thew
Edited by: Claire Haugh
Design and layout by: Nicola Sedgwick

Printed in Ireland by ColourBooks

1 3 5 7 9 8 6 4 2

Foreword

In October 2005, publisher Danny McCarthy turned down my collection of ornate Petrarchan verse, savaged my 'light-hearted' children's novel set during the biblical Slaughter of the Innocents and guffawed at the treatise on my Grand Aunt's collection of antique toenail clippers.

'They'll never sell,' he said, skilfully steepling the pages between two ashtrays and setting fire to them with the satisfaction of a man who has done the public a great service. I sat in silent stupefaction as the pages wriggled and writhed in their fiery death throes. The barman, wisely, stayed behind the bar.

'Nicola Sedgwick has an idea,' he said, finally, blowing the froth off his choco-mocha-latte decaf onto my carbonised words. They sizzled and died. 'We want you to write a book about Irish "extremes",' he said. 'You know, a quest for the "est" – highest, lowest, widest and so forth. Will you do it?'

'No,' I said, flouncing off, and then flouncing back thirty seconds later to say 'yes'. Pride is a terrible thing if you don't possess a backbone.

The book, I demanded, would have to be different to all those other tomes about Ireland with their 'amazing factoids'. For every superlative (biggest, smallest etc) I would cram in a load of other unrelated – and sometimes untrue – nuggets of information. I could be rude where I wanted, and we would aim the book at Irish people – not just tourists. It would be the Alternative Irish Miscellany, with stuff the public didn't know, might half-remember or couldn't be bothered asking about. We would call it 'Erindipity' and it would another way of amusing oneself in the bathroom. Would he agree to these demands?

'Just go away and do it,' he sighed, examining his fingernails (which could have done with my Grand Aunt's clippers).

And here it is.

Dave Kenny

Dedication

With all my love to my wife Gillian
who is – on top of everything else – my best friend.

And with love to:
Ted for the genes,
Gráinne for ironing them,
Niamh, Deirdre, Martin and Rory
for lying that they still fit me.
Also to Paul, Carmel, Margaret and Sophie Carroll,
Dominick and little Ben Lewis
for being such a lovely bunch of people.

And in memory of Nóinín Carey, Michael Long
and Richard Grainger

Acknowledgements

The worst thing about writing an acknowledgment section is that, inevitably, you're going to leave someone out – no matter how important or obvious they are.

The following (if my memory serves me right) deserve the lion's share of gratitude for their help: Danny McCarthy, Claire Haugh, Nicola Sedgwick and all at Mentor Books; the archivists of the Independent Group, *The Irish Times*, *Irish Examiner* and all the papers I've plundered; the National Library, RTÉ, Eastern Rumelian Radio, Bosco Fogarty, A Large Lemon, Various Barmen and Taxi Drivers, a Rabbit Wrangler named Clive, His Holiness The Pope, Andrew Flood, Cianán O'Sullivan, Ken, Ian, Diebs, Ringo and the hilarious Jim Connolly (not the 1916 one).

To you all, a large 'thank you' and a basket of muffins (while stocks last).

Contents

People
Best and Worst

Politest and Rudest

Youngest and Oldest

Longest, Shortest and Tallest

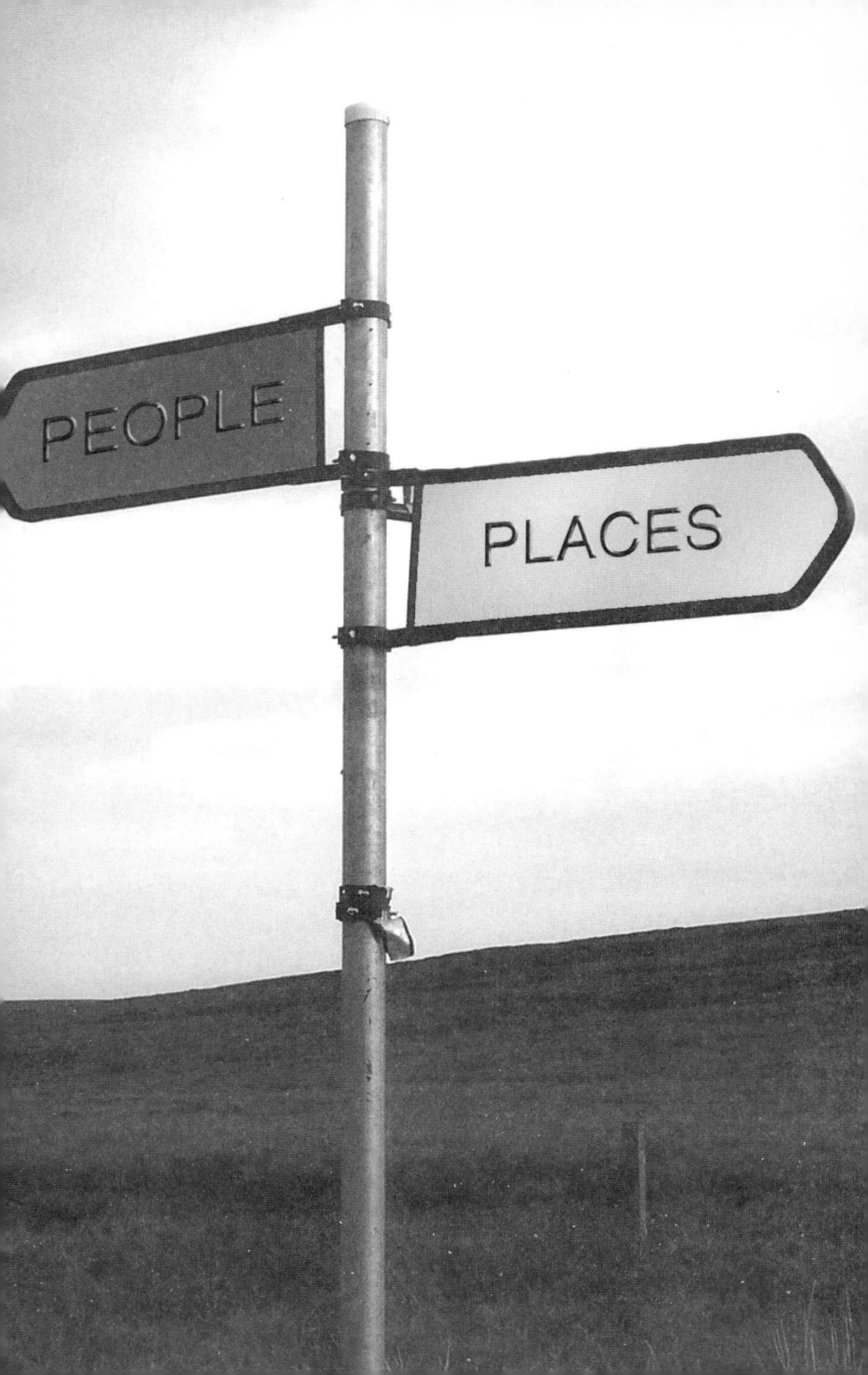
PEOPLE
PLACES

Longest and Shortest

Longest River

The longest river in Ireland is the Shannon, flowing a majestic, if somewhat squiggly, 360 km, of which 258 km is freshwater and 102 km is tidal. It is also the longest river in Ireland and Great Britain, pipping the piddling Severn in England by anything up to 32 km depending on who you read. That boast aside, the Shannon is only one eighteenth the length of the Nile (6,736 km), so don't get over-excited. It (the Shannon, not the Nile) rises east of Sligo Bay at Shannon Pot and becomes tidal above Limerick, 80 km from the open sea.

The Shannon is connected to Dublin by two waterways, the Grand Canal and the Royal Canal. One of its more interesting features is the series of lakes along its course, Loughs Allen, Ree and Derg being the biggest. One less interesting aspect is that for the most part the Shannon gloops along and is prone to both flooding and low water levels during drought.

That aside, it's a fairly hard-working river, helping to provide a lively 110 megawatts of electricity at the hydroelectric plant at **Ardnacrusha**, south of Killaloe. Ardnacrusha, by the way, was built by the German firm Siemens-Shuckert, who won the contract in 1924.

The Shannon has the delightful privilege of flowing through some of Ireland's most glamorous counties: Cavan, Leitrim, Longford, Westmeath, Clare and Limerick, the latter of which is named after a type of rhyme.

Limerick City is also known affectionately as the Treaty City due to the historical accord signed there between Patrick Sarsfield's Jacobites and the Williamites in 1691. This nickname is a touch ironic as the city was home to a long-running, seemingly endless feud at the start of the twenty-first century between rival family factions involved in criminal activities, resulting in six murders by 2006.

These figures, however, paint an unfair picture of the place when compared to the fatality list for Dublin's so-called Crumlin Drugs Gangs Feud. Nine people had been gunned down in the country's capital by the end of the same period.

Limerick people have a tendency to go mental when the Dublin media dub their metropolis 'Stab City' due to the seemingly high rate of knife attacks perpetrated there. This monicker was replaced by the quaint 'Dodge City' at the height of the aforementioned feud, further straining inter-city relations. Limerick's cause, however, wasn't helped by its own Super Mario lookalike and Minister for Defence **Willie O'Dea.** He appeared on the front page of *The Irish Times* in November 2005 – just after a double gangland slaying – pointing an unloaded gun at a cameraman at the Curragh. Which may prove that, like the Nile, which gave the world Moses, the Shannon, too, has its own fair share of basket cases.

Limerick is also famous for having Ireland's **Shortest-Lived Soviet** (more about that later) and at least two connections with the American–Indian Wars of the late nineteenth century. Both connections, coincidentally, are rugby-based. Garryowen is one of Limerick's oldest – and toughest – rugby union clubs and lent its name to the 'theme tune' of General Custer's Seventh Cavalry, who were famously slaughtered by the Sioux nation at Little Big Horn. The second connection concerns the actor **Richard Harris**, arguably Limerick's most famous son, who shot to fame in the movie *This Sporting Life* (1962) as a boorish north of England rugby league player. In that movie he (or rather his character) had six teeth removed after a clash on the pitch. Harris was, of course, only play-acting. However, in the movie *A Man Called Horse* (1970), he actually underwent the incredible rites-of-passage of a Sioux warrior for real. Proving that there is definitely 'something' in the Shannon water, he allowed himself to be hung by his man-diddies from the roof of a traditional Indian lodge. Catch Terry Wogan ever doing that.

Harris died on 26 October 2002 and his ashes were flown to his home in the Bahamas (note – not Limerick). His reputation as a hard-drinking, womanising gadabout sometimes overshadows his achievements as an actor. During his 44-year acting career he was Oscar-nominated twice – for his roles in *This Sporting Life* (1962) and *The Field* (1990) and was Emmy and BAFTA nominated once each. Unlike fellow Celtic boozer **Richard Burton**, whose body failed to keep up with his excessive lifestyle, Harris not only survived until the age of 72 but also managed to resurrect his career at the age of 60 (as the Bull McCabe), going on to scale the celluloid heights with performances as Marcus Aurelius in *Gladiator* (2000) and Professor Dumbledore in two of the Harry Potter movies. It was during the shooting of the former film that Harris became friends with New Zealand[1] charmer **Russell Crowe**.

'General Maximus' was so taken with Harris and upset by his death that he flew over – in his honour – for an International match between the Wallabies and Ireland at Lansdowne Road. His mood wasn't lightened by the sight of the Aussies being beaten in double scores (18–9).

Crowe also headed to Limerick, where he visited numerous pubs frequented by Harris and in Charlie St George's scribbled an emotional tribute on a pub serviette in which he declared his undying affection for

[1] Contrary to the widely-held belief that he is Australian.

his generous-spirited friends.

While in Ireland he also wrote a song on a beer mat respectfully titled 'Mr Harris'. The lyrics include the words 'Emerald', 'Glorious Green' and 'Irish Hearts'. Some have cruelly suggested that it would have been more appropriate to write it on a sick-bag instead. Those people were not in attendance however when he recited it to a crowd of 1,500 delighted locals at the unveiling of a statue of his hero in Kilkee, County Clare in September 2006.

Crowe – who was arrested in 2005 for hopping a telephone off a New York bell-hop's head – was on his best behaviour during his jaunt and appeared to enjoy his few pints of Guinness. Local lore has it that he didn't even frown when he was refused an after-hours drink in Nancy's Bar in the city. Where else but in Limerick would someone be brave enough to do that?

The Shannon (remember the Shannon?) is also the only Irish river after which Irish–American parents are likely to name their daughters. Who, after all, is going to name their child 'Liffey' or 'Barrow' or indeed 'Suck'?

Apart from flash-in-the-pan Hollywood starlet Shannon Doherty, all American girls named Shannon have huge hairstyles, large bottoms and a fondness for wearing white polo necks under Aran sweaters.

Lee Majors is named after a river in Cork.

INTERESTING FACTS

- The Shannon is named after the Irish goddess Sionnan.
- The third longest river in Ireland is the Suir (183 km).
- Mulgrave Street in Limerick contains two hospitals, a jail and a lunatic asylum and is nicknamed Calamity Avenue.
- In rugby tactics, a Garryowen is where a team kick the ball high in the air and descend *en masse* upon the halfwit who tries to catch it.
- Other Limerick celebrities include Eamon De Valera, *Angela's Ashes* author Frank McCourt, (Sir) Terry Wogan and Rose Fitzgerald, mother of John F Kennedy.

Shortest River

The shortest river in Ireland is the Corrib, which flows from its namesake lough through Galway City and out into Galway Bay. The Corrib also has the unique distinction of being the shortest river in Europe at a tiny 6.4 km from lake to sea. However, like most Galway Shams it may be small but it's powerfully built – especially after it's been raining, which it does all the time in Galway. As a result it's popular with whitewater kayak enthusiasts and Culchies needing to be turbo-cleaned.

The Corrib may be the shortest river and the Shannon the longest river in the Republic, but if you want to get really technical about it, the longest river in Northern Ireland is the Bann at 128 km and the shortest would be **The Six Mile Water**, if it wasn't in fact 32 km long. An indirect tributary of the Bann, it got its name from a group of Norman soldiers who miscalculated the march from Carrickfergus Castle to Ballyclare in the late twelfth century.

If the Normans were all as thick as those chaps, then they must have been totally confused when they kept coming across the Blackwater River wherever they roamed around the rest of the country. There's a Blackwater in the North, in Munster and in County Meath. And if that's not confusing enough there's also a Bann in County Wicklow and a River Derry . . . and a Hollywood (although it's spelled differently from the Holywood in County Down on account of Northerners being more God-fearing than anyone else and movies being the work of the Devil or Neil Jordan). And there's a Bray with a movie studio – Ardmore – which is not the same as Bray Studios, Windsor, England where all the Hammer horror movies were produced. And isn't the north of Bray (supposedly in County Wicklow) in County Dublin?

There's a picture emerging here. Could it be that Wicklow wants to be somewhere else? Riding to hounds with its Anglo friends in the Black North or the Jackeen East, perhaps? Or maybe it just wants to get away from the wrath of the **Dargle**, the longest/shortest river (19 km) running through Bray?

The Dargle has a nasty habit of bursting its banks, and over the past 100 years, there have been four major floods in Little Bray, causing one death from drowning (in 1905) and massive property damage. In between, there have been numerous less-destructive, but nevertheless unpleasant, inundations.

The last 'biggy' was on the night of 25 August 1986 during **Hurricane Charlie**, when the Dargle whooshed across vast areas of the town, rising to over two metres in places. The Civil Defence had to be called away from whatever the Civil Defence do when there are no natural disasters or invasions, and 500 people were evacuated. The Order of Malta were there as well to ensure there was no shortage of smelling salts and sticking plasters.

Of course, none of this would have happened if Bray had been built on the River Corrib – it being the shortest river in Ireland and all that.

INTERESTING FACTS

- A survey published on 22 March 2006, revealed that one third of Irish rivers and lakes were polluted, with County Monaghan topping the lake list.
- 20 million eels swim into the River Bann in Northern Ireland each spring to breed.

- The River Foyle is the fastest flowing river in Europe and has the continent's only double-decker bridge (at Craigavon).

- Counties Galway and Wicklow are famous for having the most popular amusements on the west and east coasts – at Salthill and Bray respectively and the world's highest concentration of 'skangers' ram-riding each other in the dodgems at any one time.

- The author's underpants blew out of a boarding house window in the Isle of Man during Hurricane Charlie. All of them. True story!

Shortest-Lived Soviet

Post-Easter-Rising Ireland was a hot bed of labour militancy, with 100 workers' 'Soviets' springing up around the country between the years 1917 and 1923. The most famous of these was the Limerick Soviet, which was founded on 14 April 1919, following the funeral of IRA Volunteer Bobby Byrnes.

Byrnes – who was also active in the Trade Unions – had been shot while escaping from Limerick Union Hospital on 6 April 1919. Two RIC men were killed during his dash for freedom and the British authorities introduced Martial Law to clamp down on attendance at his funeral three days later. Extra soldiers and police were deployed to set up checkpoints, and anyone wanting to enter the city could only do so with a special permit. In response, labour leaders decided to strike. On 12 April employees at the Condensed Milk Company stopped working.

As the British are a race renowned for their love of condensed milk, there was general consternation and two days later when a general strike was called – possibly affecting the distribution of tea and cucumber sandwiches in the city – the crown forces were apopleptic.

15,000 workers out of a population of almost 40,000 joined the strike, with only essential public utilities, the banks and civil servants operating. Food producers were also exempted. That week Limerick was full of hundreds of journalists covering the attempt by **Major Woods** to fly across the Atlantic and within days the Limerick Soviet had gained worldwide attention and support. As it looked like the strikers were in it for the long haul, panic buying of food kicked in and the Commies ordered the bakers back to work and fixed the price of 'basics' (milk, butter etc). Thousands of tons of grain on board a docked ship were 'liberated' and depots were set up outside the city to receive food donations, which were smuggled in to the hungry workers. The Soviet issued travel passes to thousands travelling on the city's transportation system and even set up its own 'Mint', issuing its own currency. All things being unequal (as they say in left wing politics), the strike appeared to be a great success. Not for long though. Soon opposition from the authorities and the Church swayed people away from the cause and on

24 April the strike was called off. It had lasted 10 days, as opposed to the 80-odd years of Russian Communism.

At this point you could be forgiven for thinking that Limerick's history is all about gun feuds and Marxist revolutions. Therefore it might surprise you to learn that the first game of Polo – the current Prince of Wales' favourite sport – ever staged outside of Asia, was played in Limerick in 1868 by members of the British Cavalry's 10th Hussars. And, unlike their fearsome counterparts in Afghanistan, no human heads were used as balls.

The genesis of **Polo Mints**, by the way, has nothing to do with the sport, or Limerick for that matter. The name derives from the word 'Polar', describing the popular sweets' fresh flavour. It would be churlish to point out here that Polo is a mint with a hole, while Limerick – at the time of the Soviet – was a hole with a Mint.

INTERESTING FACTS

- The first recorded Polo tournament took place in 600BC when the Turkomans beat the Persians. (Do you really need to know the score?) Back then the rules consisted of 'knock lumps off your opponents and score the most goals'. (This is probably why it caught on so quickly in Limerick.)

  The first set of written rules for the game were created by an Irishman, Captain John Watson of the 13th Hussars in the mid–nineteenth century. And, what's more, the All Ireland Club in Dublin (1872), is the world's second oldest Polo club outside of India. And you thought it was all Pimms and Johnny English types.

Shortest Place Name

Inch (County Kerry)

Longest Place Name

Sixmilebridge (County Clare). Doesn't have quite the same ring when converted to the metric measurement Nine.point.six.five.kilometrebridge.

(Real) Longest Place Name

Muckanaghederdauhaulia (County Galway)

Longest Stretch Of Stone Wall

Inis Mór, one of the Aran Islands off the coast of Galway, has the longest stretch of unbroken dry stone wall in Ireland, measuring 9.65 km. The combined length of all the walls on the island is 13,679 km as determined by the Department of Dry Stone Wall Measuring 2002.

Smallest and Largest

Smallest County (With Biggest Stars)

The smallest county is County Louth at 821 sq km – Cork is eight times its size.

Lying 64 km north of Dublin on the east coast (or as they say in Dundalk, 'owen-leee an owwww-er fhraum Dawhblin'), County Louth is the last hitching post before you hit the Northern badlands. Being wedged between Dublin's Northside and County Down's tight little backside, the inhabitants of this bijou county have developed what is absolutely the most horrible hybrid accent in Ireland. Combining the worst elements of both – the swaggering dis-and-dat of de Dubs with the whine of the North – it is best imagined as the sound made by a bullock being force-fed ice lollies while having its goolies pounded with a mallet. The only Louth people who don't sound like this (most of the time) are Dundalk's finest export, **The Corrs**. Superstar Bono once likened their sound to being the loudest whisper in pop; others say this charming happy-go-lucky Dundalk quartet sound every syllable like happy little Irish fairies. Happy, happy, happy little Irish fairies . . . on smack . . . and after winning the Lotto.

The happy, lovely smiling Corrs even *look* like happy little fairies, except for the one who shaves. He just looks a bit confused. By summer 2006 the singing siblings had sold a staggering 30 million records, beguiling the world with their brand of happy fairy/sad fairy Irishy pop music, not to mention their good looks. Front-woman Andrea is forever topping the Most Wanted lists in British lads' magazines, which is probably down to the fact that despite all the mystical, Bohemian posturing in her videos, the raven-haired singer still has a whiff of bog smoke about her. The Brits like that sort of thing – so much so that they gave the Corrs a clatter of OBEs in 2005 for services to the British music industry. This news didn't go down well in El Paso Country, which is not renowned for its love of the Queen – as Ian Paisley's deputy in the DUP discovered when he invaded it in 1986.

On 7 August 1986 **Peter Robinson** led a party of 500 loyalist yahoos into the metropolis of Clontibret, County Monaghan in protest at the Anglo–Irish Agreement. Some of the crowd entered the Garda station in the village, assaulted two officers and then held a quasi-military drill in the square. Monaghan, like Louth, is a small border county and so it didn't take these Loyal Sons of Ulster long to leg it back up north. Robinson, however, was arrested, tried and fined IR£17,500 in Dundalk (€22,200) for this memorable incident.

Some say the nickname 'The Wee County' is down to the smell of the place while most agree it has to do with 'wee' being Northish for 'small'. Whatever about its size, Louth has one of the densest populations in the country, outside of Dublin. It also has a lot of people living in it. In fact, at 105,000-plus people, it has almost twice the population of **Laois** – a county almost twice its size. Laois and Louth share the same distinction of being in the L group of counties. This grouping, which also comprises **Longford, Leitrim** and **Limerick**, is normally best avoided. This is because Longford Town (Dog Food Capital of Ireland) would be a one-horse town, if the inhabitants hadn't eaten it; Leitrim is the Country and Western Capital of Ireland, while Limerick . . . well let's not say any more about Limerick, other than that some of its more infamous citizens are currently leashed in Laois – Portlaoise, to be precise, and its 203-bed prison.

Laois is also where **Andrea Corr**'s fledgling acting career hit its first bump in 2006. Filming on the movie *Knife Edge* was cancelled in Stradbally due to money problems. Andrea was signed on to star alongside arch-Englishman **Charles Dance**, but never even got to film her scenes. Prior to this her credits included *Evita* (1996), *The Boys and Girl from County Clare* (2003), *The Bridge* (2006) and *Broken Thread* (2006). She also played Sharon Rabbitte in *The Commitments* (1991) – a role later reprised by Tina Kellegher in *The Snapper* (1993), starring **Colm Meaney** as 'The Da'. Meaney also starred alongside Andrea in *The Boys and Girl from County Clare.*

In *Layer Cake* (2004) Meaney starred opposite **Daniel Craig**, who took over as James Bond from **Pierce Brosnan**, who was born in Drogheda[2] on 16 May 1953.

Apart from his good looks (voted The Sexiest Man Alive by *People Magazine* in 2001), his acting skills, and the fact that he was born in County Louth, Pierce has something else in common with Andrea – an OBE, which he was awarded in 2003. Being 1.83 m in height, Pierce OBE towers over tiny Andrea OBE, who is the smallest of the Corrs at 1.55 m tall and likes to perform in her bare feet.

With this in mind, County Louth can proudly boast that it may be the smallest county in Ireland, but it's given birth to two of the world's tallest and smallest stars.

INTERESTING FACTS

- After the release of *Die Another Day* (2002), Pierce was approached in a Dublin pub by a fan asking to shake his hand. After complying he was amused to hear the wag say to his chums, 'That's the closest my hand will ever get to Halle Berry's arse.'

- Pierce earned $42m (€33 m) for his roles in the 007 movies, which could have been renamed 042 if they had been shot in the County Louth area.

- From 1959 to 1961 the Dundalk Engineering Company produced the Heinkel Kabine Bubble Car (remember them?) out of the cockpits from

---

[2] And you thought he was born in Navan, County Meath.

old Jerry bombers. The Dundalk versions were known as Heinkel Irelands.

- Carlow (at 896 sq km) is the second smallest county in Ireland and Dublin (919 sq km) is the third smallest, yet the latter is home to one third of the country's population (up to 1.2 million). Dublin is also the 12,063rd most popular surname in the United States.

- County Louth is home to a Jumping Church. The chapel at Kilmedock gets its name from the west gable wall, which seems to have leaped off its foundations and is now inside the nave. Local lore says the wall jumped so the body of an excommunicated murderer was no longer buried within the building. Some say a storm in 1715 was the real reason for the wall moving. Others say the church was just trying to hop it out of County Louth. The latter sounds most plausible.

Largest County

Cork. Or so they keep telling everybody.

Largest Lake That Also Happens To Be An Entrance To Hell

Ulster's Lough Neagh (380 sq km) is the largest lake in Ireland and Britain. It's approximately 32 km long and 14km wide, very shallow around the edges and has an average depth of nearly 10 metres, sloping off to 24 metres at its deepest point. Bordered by five of the six counties of Northern Ireland – Antrim, Armagh, Derry, Down and Tyrone – it is fed by six major rivers, which drain about 43% of Northern Ireland, plus part of the stony grey soil of County Monaghan.

Extraordinarily for a parcel of land its size, the lough is privately owned by the **Earls of Shaftesbury**. This only became known in 2005 and caused no end of consternation as the lake, which supplies 40% of the region's drinking water, was widely believed to be the property of the state. Those old Northern Planters, where would we be without them?

There are legends galore (or *go leor* as they say in Irish) surrounding Lough Neagh's construction, the most famous being how it was formed when **Fionn mac Cumhaill** scooped up some of the land and tossed it at a Scottish rival. He missed, and the chunk of earth landed in the sea, creating the Isle of Man and the large divot that is Lough Neagh. Considering the Lough is only 380 sq km and the Isle of Man is 572 sq km, either Fionn was lying about his marvellous feat or he was just very bad at maths.

There is also another legend concerning a holy tree on the Tyrone shore of the lough, which was said to bring good fortune to those who hammered coins into its trunk. It eventually died of metal poisoning.

At 176 sq km, the second largest lake in Ireland (and the biggest in the Republic) is **Lough Corrib** which feeds Ireland's shortest river, the Corrib. The third is **Lough Derg** in Munster, which is a strapping 119 sq km and is not to be confused with Ireland's other **Lough Derg** in Donegal. The latter, although only covering about 809 hectares, is the biggest lake in that county and therefore can lay claim to the title of Largest Lake That Also Happens To Be An Entrance To (cue organ music) . . . Hell.

This other 'Red Lake' has been renowned for its European Christian pilgrimages since the sixth century and lies north of the village of Pettigo. **Station Island**, the location of 'St Patrick's Purgatory' on the lake was deemed so important in medieval times that it was among the principal landmarks on maps of Ireland. It was, for example, the only Irish site named on a world map of 1492.

So what did early Christians find so attractive about this bleak, boggy, rain-lashed part of the world? It was the opportunity to descend – like St Patrick – into a cave on the island (which was the second[3] entrance to the Underworld) and experience the secrets of the Afterlife. These consisted of stinking pits, souls nailed to wheels, extremes of temperature, demons etc and so forth. A virtuous – and pretty damned brave person – could head to Purgatory and have their soul purged of the stains of sin before returning to life. After doing this they would not have to revisit Purgatory after death. They would have to pass through Pettigo again on their way home though.

With its incessant rain, Lough Derg is a textbook Irish Purgatory and each year tens of thousands arrive at the end of May for the traditional pilgrimage. The faithful must be at least 15 years of age, healthy and able to walk and kneel unaided. The pilgrimage is a three-day fast,

---

[3] The first was the pyrotechnically superior and eminently showy Mount Etna in Sicily. Even when descending to hell the Italians have 'flare'.

incorporating a 24-hour vigil, and pilgrims are allowed only one meal of dry toast, oatcakes and black tea or Lough Derg soup (hot water with salt and pepper). The central part of the pilgrimage involves people walking barefoot and kneeling between 'stations' at which they recite repeated prayers.

Pebbles and gravel stick to the visitors' feet and the sharp rocks of the penitential beds have tormented many poor soles over the years. Is it any wonder then that, in centuries past when the 'tour' was up to 15 days long, many devotees had horrible visions?

> **Pebbles and gravel stick to the visitors' feet and the sharp rocks of the penitential beds have tormented many poor soles over the years.**

Then there is **Croagh Patrick** in County Mayo for those who would rather ascend to Heaven than descend to Purgatory for their sins. Every year on the last Sunday in July, thousands of people climb the 765 m 'Reek' during the night (in bare feet if possible) and try not to fall off. According to legend, Saint Patrick – who covered a lot of ground in his day – fasted on the mountain's summit for the 44 days of Lent in 441AD. When he was through, he reportedly threw a bell down the side of the mountain, banishing all the snakes of Ireland. As there were none there in the first place, and as he had just built a church on an empty stomach, he might be forgiven for hallucinating a little.

Lough Derg and the slopes of Croagh Patrick aside, the real entrance to Hell is Portarlington. And if you don't know why, you deserve to wind up there.

INTERESTING FACTS

- In the early 1990s, a gold seam was discovered running straight through Croagh Patrick. A number of Dublin entrepreneurs wanted to develop it as an 'environmentally sensitive' mine but the locals have managed to keep it unspoiled.
- Lough Derg ('Dearg' or 'Red' Lake) is reputed to get its name from the blood-colouring of the water after Saint Patrick killed a huge dragon that had terrorised the countryside. Strangely, no trace of that dragon – like the snakes – has ever been found.
- The police station in Dungannon, County Tyrone – one of the counties lapped by Lough Neagh – should actually overlook the Khyber Pass in India. During the nineteenth century the plans for this fortress were sent by mistake to Ireland instead of the Sub Continent.
- Croagh Patrick is called 'The Reek' because of the whang off the pilgrims' feet.

Smallest Church

As every student of modern Ireland knows, when the inhabitants of this island are not stick-fighting with the next village, tugging their forelocks to English tourists or climbing Croagh Patrick, they are either in the pub or at Mass. In the past – and especially during the time of the Penal Laws – the Holy Liturgy was often celebrated on a rock in a back field or behind a hedge, but today most Irish people prefer to worship indoors. This is why there are so many churches in Ireland (757,003 approx). Of these, the most modern all belong to the Pope and the older ones to the Church of Ireland, due to the Reformation, where it was agreed the Protestants would get all the best churches and the Catholics could keep the pubs. Wart-faced Oliver Cromwell tried to undo this deal when he arrived in 1649 but the publicans went underground and wandered the countryside disguised as privet hedges, dispensing drinks to the natives. Thus was born the tradition of bush-drinking that is still continued to this day in Blanchardstown, the Noggin and Carlow.

The Irish Protestants, too, managed to ride out the Cromwellian storm and held on to their churches, keeping not only the most ancient, but also the biggest – **St Patrick's Cathedral in Dublin**. This magnificent building dates from 1191 when Archbishop of Dublin John Comyn (a sour old git) raised the original, wooden, Celtic St Patrick's Church on the site to the status of Cathedral. Work on the new building started in 1225 and took 30 years to complete. St Patrick's then remained untouched for 600 years until the Victorians got their hands on it. Most of the current building now actually dates from the 1870s when renovations took place to stop it from falling down.

True to form, the builders forgot to keep records of the

original scale of the Cathedral and now nobody knows how much is medieval and how much is Victorian. What does remain is the store of colourful stories about the place, such as that of laugh-a-minute Cromwell stabling his horse in its nave to show his disrespect for the Anglican religion. In 1713 Jonathan Swift, the great champion of Dublin's poor, became Dean of St Patrick's and remained there until 1745 during which time he gave the world *Gulliver's Travels* amongst other literary wonders.

St Patrick's also added the phrase 'chancing your arm' to the Dubliner's lexicon, when the Earl of Kildare cut a hole in the Cathedral door and thrust his arm through it in an effort to call a truce with the Earl of Ormond in 1492.

What **St Brendan the Navigator** would have made of cutting holes in holy churches is anyone's guess. The poor state of the door to his cathedral in Clonfert, County Galway led the Heritage Council to commission a conservation plan in 2000. The restoration took place 1,441 years after the Sailing Saint built the first church on the site. In fact, St Brendan's Cathedral (drum-roll please), is the Oldest Living Church in Ireland with an unbroken history of public worship, which considering the amount of times it's been attacked is quite an achievement. Being situated close to the Shannon it's had its fair share of Viking marauders, but the first written record of it being burnt dates from 1164. It was re-built in 1167 and then burnt again in 1179 and re-built for a second time. In spite of all those conflagrations part of the nave from

908AD is still in place.

Due to the previously mentioned church/pub accord St Brendan's Cathedral is in Anglican hands and many fine members of that congregation have, over the years, contributed to its upkeep as one of the most important Christian sites in Ireland. The last devastating fire in the immediate environs of the cathedral broke out in the Bishop's Palace in Christmas 1954. For three years prior to this the property had been home to Sir Oswald Mosley, former leader of the British Union of Fascists. The building was destroyed (Hellfire, anyone?) and the Mosleys left in 1955 giving the palace, grounds and woodland to the diocese. The house has been derelict ever since.

In contrast, there have been no fires of any great merit attached to the history of **Ireland's Oldest Catholic Church**, St Patrick's Cathedral (another one), which can be found off George's Street in Waterford City. The present structure has been in operation since 1750, but prior to its erection a Fr Edmond Everard is recorded as having ministered there in 1704 – a good 1,209 years after St Patrick was reputed to have built his first church at Druim Saileach (Willow Ridge) in Armagh. The present cathedrals (one Catholic and one Protestant) in Armagh date from the nineteenth century, should you be a glutton for details.

While no one has ever sat down to work it out, it is estimated that the combined floor space of these two cathedrals, plus that of the St Patrick's Cathedrals in Dublin and Waterford, is 2,673 times that of

The Smallest Church in Ireland.

This dinky little chapel can be found in the picturesque town of Portbradden on the north Antrim coast. In marked counterpoint to the Giant's Causeway, which is only down the road, the church is a modest 1.5 m high by 3 m long by 2 m wide and is dedicated to St Gobhnan, the patron saint of builders.

INTERESTING FACTS

- The funerals of two presidents, Douglas Hyde and Erskine Childers, took place in St Patrick's Cathedral in Dublin in 1949 and 1974 respectively. At President Hyde's funeral, the entire government and opposition, bar Noel Browne and Erskine Childers, stayed out in the foyer of the church due to the Catholic ban on members entering Protestant churches. Childers, by the way, was the first President to die in office.

- Mass has been celebrated every Sunday in Ballintubber Abbey, County Mayo since 1216.

- The 'bullaun stone' in St. Matthew's Church on the Woodvale Road in Belfast, is believed to have the power to cure warts, spots and acne. Pity someone didn't smack Cromwell over the head with it.

- Dublin's second, older Anglican Cathedral is Christ Church, which was founded by Dúnán, the first bishop of Dublin and Sitric, the Norse

King of the city, in 1030. It was originally intended that St Patrick's, a secular cathedral, would replace Christ Church but this was resisted by the latter resulting in the unusual situation of the two churches both possessing the rights of 'Cathedral of the Diocese'. Whatever about all that, the really interesting thing about Christ Church is that during the sixteenth and seventeenth centuries its crypt was used as a pub, as a letter of 1633 shows: 'The vaults from one end of the minster to the other are made into tippling houses for beer, wine and tobacco.' Beat that, St Patrick's.

Highest
and Lowest

Highest Waterfall

The highest waterfall in Ireland – and Britain – is 121 m and cascades into the Dargle at Powerscourt Demesne in Enniskerry, County Wicklow. The estate has been a favourite with visitors for the past 200 years, with possibly its most illustrious being **King George IV** in 1821. As a special honour, the Powerscourt family had a special viewing platform built near the waterfall and, in order to create a greater spectacle, constructed a dam above the falls. However, the king spent too long enjoying the hospitality at Powerscourt House 5 km away and never saw the waterfall because when the dam was removed the huge swoosh of water swept the viewing platform away.

Whatever about George and his dammed waterfall, a far more interesting 'Highest' is the world record set by Michael O'Brien on 26 September 2002. Michael passed the Highest Sheaf Tossing mark with his throw of 18 m and 33 cm high for a 3.62 kg sheaf at the National Ploughing Championships, Ballacolla, County Laois. What a tosser.

INTERESTING FACTS

- In 1858 the seventh Viscount Powerscourt successfully introduced the Japanese Sikka deer to Ireland. He then proceeded to hunt them down and shoot them for his tea.

Highest Mountain

That would be Carrauntoohil in County Kerry's Macgillycuddy Reeks. It stands at 1,041 m. Only in Kerry would you find a mountain range that sounds like an insult.

Lowest Pub

No other country on the planet is more obsessed with facts and figures about Public Houses than Ireland. Where else would you find records for Oldest Pub, Biggest Pub, Most Expensive Pub, Rudest Pub, Best Pint Pub, Cabbagiest Smelling Pub, Just Plain Smelly Pub, Roughest Pub, Toughest Pub, Plushest Pub, Gayest Pub, Mankiest Pub etc (other than Wales, and who cares about

Wales)? The Irish are born genetically pre-programmed with the urge to wink sagaciously over a pint glass at the nearest tourist and inform him of the special status of the drinking emporium he has just entered.

So to satisfy this base need, here are a few of the record-holders:

Biggest Pub: An English 'Stag Weekend' website[4] claims this can be found in the Arlington Hotel off O'Connell Bridge in Dublin. And they should know. However, many would argue that the entire Temple Bar area holds this title. It's got a 'bar' in its name at any rate.

Smallest Pub: The Dawson Lounge off Stephen's Green in Dublin. This little gem is the size of a big sitting room with a bar in the middle. Great for eavesdropping.

Culchiest Pub: Robert Reid's, Frenchman's Lane in Dublin. Facing Store Street Garda Station and Busaras, lunchtimes here are a veritable honey trap – or bacon and cabbage trap – for culchie guards and clod-hoppers getting the bus back down the country. Great pub despite these incursions.

Just Plain Smelly Pub: We can't name this Dublin establishment for legal reasons. Think of a toilet that looks like Buffalo Bill's boudoir in *Silence of the Lambs* (1991) and smells like a fishmonger's jockstrap.

Lowest Pub: The Cellar Bar in the Merrion Hotel in Dublin.

The other top factoids beloved of pub enthusiasts are 'Highest' and 'Oldest'. Let's deal with the latter first.

Every publican in the country wants his ale house to be the nation's most ancient and so attract the maximum

---

[4] www.lastnightoffreedom.co.uk

amount of tourists – which is understandable, even laudable. Over the years there have been countless rows about which bar holds this title, but the three main contenders are Grace Neill's in Donaghadee, County Down, The Brazen Head in Dublin and Sean's Bar in Athlone, County Westmeath.

According to those people who keep track of these things, Grace Neill's is the **Oldest Licenced Pub** in Ireland and first opened in 1611 as the King's Arms. Grace Neill was a regular patron of the pub who got her last orders in 1918 at the sprightly age of 98. The pub was renamed in her honour and local lore has it that her (benign) ghost is still in the building[5].

In 1613, The Brazen Head got its licence as a coaching inn, but it has a verifiable history stretching all the way back to 1198. Even its location hints at its great age – Bridge Street, on which it is situated, is only a stone's throw from the original hurdle ford of Ye Olde Dublinia and is within the medieval walls of the city. The provenance of its name is a mystery, but Frank Hopkins relates how one of Ireland's two other 'Brazen Head' taverns got its name in his hugely entertaining *Rare Old Dublin*. The story goes that an unfortunate red-haired prostitute was watching hostilities during the 1691 Siege of Limerick from her brothel window (as you do) when a cannonball took her head off. When a new pub was built on the site in 1794 it was called The Sign of The Brazen Head.

The Brazen Head in Dublin has its own military associations and was, variously, the meeting place for the

---

[5] They'll never be low on spirits, then.

United Irishmen, Robert Emmet's hideout in 1803 and a rendezvous for Michael Collins. It is mentioned in James Joyce's *Ulysses*, while Mulligans of Poolbeg Street in Dublin provides the backdrop for the story 'Counterparts' in *Dubliners*.

Mulligans, which is **The Best Pint Pub**, might also have been considered a past candidate for **The Rudest Pub** award. The author once overheard a Californian tourist asking for a Gaelic coffee, only to be informed by the barman that he 'didn't do cocktails'. We say 'might also have been' because the late gentlemen in question revelled in portraying himself as gruff but was actually an extremely decent chap who provided the author with enough 'slates' to roof the Pro-Cathedral. God bless him.

Contrary to popular belief, John Mulligan didn't start his business on Poolbeg Street, but in a house on Thomas Street beside the Cornmarket in 1782. His name has adorned the pub's exterior only since 1854, which is not nearly as far back as the birthday of the granddaddy of them all – Sean's Bar in Athlone.

Athlone, or Áth Luain, translates into 'Luain's Ford' after a Westmeathian who made his living by guiding travellers over the treacherous waters of the Shannon. He was also the first publican on this spot and opened an inn beside the river in the first century AD. He must have served good pints, because over the years a settlement grew up around his hostel, culminating in King Turlough O'Connor building the first wooden castle at the site in 1129.

Sean's Bar now occupies the inn established by Luain and has a documented history of all its innkeepers right back to 1600 when it was known as the Three Blackamoor Heads. Any lingering doubts about its age were dispelled in 1970 when, during renovations, the walls were found to be made of wattle and wicker and dated back to the ninth century.

Coincidentally, it's worth noting that the three oldest pubs in Ireland have all had anatomical references in their names at some stage – four heads (black and brazen) and a King's arms. Or maybe not.

INTERESTING FACTS

- Another pub with a body part in its name is the Hole In The Wall on Blackhorse Avenue. It was so named after the Victorian tradition of passing drinks out through a hole in the wall of the Phoenix Park to the soldiers garrisoned nearby.
- John F Kennedy went on the batter in Mulligan's in 1945 when he was working for the Hearst organisation.

Highest Pub

It must be something to do with the lack of oxygen making the booze kick in quicker, but there is nothing the true Irishman likes better than getting twisted on top of a mountain. To cater for this, over the centuries publicans have competed to build ever higher boozers – a sort of 'spaced race' if you will – the last being the **Gravity Bar** at the Guinness Storehouse in Dublin.

Standing a wobbly seven stories tall, it is the Highest Bar in any city in Ireland. However, it is only a footstool compared to the towering bar stool that is **Johnnie Fox's Pub** in the Dublin Mountains.

Fox's dates back to the rebellious year of 1798 and is perched precariously atop picturesque Glencullen. It's a landmark house, serves good food and is a staple with the thousands of tourists who flock there every year to say they've stamped on a few brain cells in 'Ireland's Highest Pub'. But is it really Ireland's Highest Pub? Possibly not.

Johnnie Fox's is located at an elevation of approximately 281 m above sea level, which makes it the highest bar in the Republic unless someone has dragged a few kegs up the side of Carrauntoohil since this book was published.

There's another pub on the island of Ireland, however, which claims to be located even higher up in the clouds. **The Ponderosa** in the Glenshane Pass through the Sperrin Mountains, near Dungiven, County Derry is said to be at 304.8 m above sea level. If this is the case, then it's 23.8 m higher than Johnnie Fox's and can legitimately claim to be the highest bar in the country. Even if it isn't, the Ponderosa (surely they should have called it the High Chaparral?) has another claim to fame. The former farmhouse featured in Gerald Seymour's novel *Harry's Game,* which was made into a TV movie in 1982 with a theme tune by Clannad (the Brennan family).

Old Mr Brennan, Leo, coincidentally owns Leo's Tavern in Gweedore, County Donegal. Located less than 76 m above sea level, it is Definitely Not Ireland's Highest Pub.

INTERESTING FACTS

- Singing Dundalk pharmacist Patrick McMahon, who passed away in June 2006, entered the *Guinness Book of Records* in 1958 when he hit the highest note of a tenor's highest octave.

- All day food in Irish pubs is a relatively new thing. Prior to the arrival of pub grub in the 1990s publicans believed their customers wouldn't want to waste their money on anything other than drink. Preoccupied with how to keep their customers thirsty and stop them from going home to their tea, they hit upon the American idea of providing bowls of salted (and germ-encrusted) peanuts, but this proved too costly and eventually the drinker had to pay for these snacks. Then, in 1954, the peanut was overthrown in a new taste revolution – the arrival of the crisp. Tayto flavoured crisps were invented by Joe Murphy at his premises on O'Rahilly's Parade off Moore Street in Dublin, and his Cheese and Onion brand are still the standard fare in most Irish pubs. While Salt and Vinegar are the height of fine dining, most publicans reckon they don't compliment the taste of drink. Which is a fair point. Have you ever eaten a salt and vinegar sandwich?

Best and Worst

Best Place To Wipe Out Northern Ireland

Silent Valley, County Down.

Here's the scenario: you're a mad Orangeman fixated with the possibility that some equally mad Republican is spending all his time devising new ways of wiping you and your Rangers-loving brethren off the map. Every street you march down you see brooding, shadowy figures rending their Rosary beads and behaving disgracefully as you attempt to exercise your cultural rights. You've seen a doctor, you know it's not that your bowler hat is too tight. You are NOT paranoid – THEY REALLY ARE OUT TO GET YOU. You would move mountains to keep Ulster in the Red Hands of its loyal sons, wouldn't you?

Nervous Unionists moved more than one mountain in 1924–25. As the Boundary Commission carved up the new Ireland, they shifted the entire Mourne Mountain range (207 sq km of spectacularly beautiful County Down) north of El Paso, because of fears that Dev and the boys might attempt to poison the water supply. As Orangemen generally prefer a nice cup of tea to hard liquor, they felt they were more at risk than their porter-swilling 'Taigue' neighbours in this respect.

In 1924 the people of **Newry**, in the heart of Mourne country, wrote to chairman Justice Richard Feetham's commission requesting that their town be included in the South. But Newry – which at the time was 75% Nationalist – was refused as the area is also home to the province's biggest reservoir, Silent Valley.

No one in the history of Silent Valley has ever attempted to poison its cool clear waters, for two simple reasons – it would be both an incredibly hard and incredibly stupid thing to do. Feetham bought it though.

He also believed the Unionist line about Beleek in Fermanagh posing another watery threat to the North's security. Nationalist townsfolk there were so confident that they would be heading south of the new border that they even brought in the Free State's school inspectors – and so they were most surprised to wake up one morning on the 'wrong' side. This was on the basis that if Fermanagh was left in the South the lakes could be used to flood the area. Evidently the Loyal Few who believed this had spent too much time in Sunday school learning about Noah's Ark.

The Commission also dealt a few blows to the Unionists of Donegal who wrote asking for the county to remain in the Union only to see the town of Pettigo being divided, north and south. Protestants in Cavan and Monaghan, likewise, petitioned to no avail. All three counties hold Orange marches each year and the names Cecil and Doris still abound there.

In fact, the town of **Ballybofey** is famous for its annual 'Whistling Sandy Festival' (pronounced 'Whisssstling tttssSandy Fessssstival'). Scores of old men in bowlers sashay across the border each year on 10 July to compete in the 'Sibilant Stakes', as it is believed that you are not a true Orangeman if you can't whistle and speak at the same time, while making your mouth look tighter than a polar bear's bum in a blizzard.

> . . . the town of **Ballybofey is famous for its annual 'Whistling Sandy Festival' (pronounced 'Whisssstling tttssSandy Fessssstival').**

'That'ssss tsimply tsplendid, young mon. tSome more tsponge cake, tCedric?' etc and so forth.

INTERESTING FACTS

- Slieve Donard (852 m) is the highest mountain in the North.
- Northerners love nothing more than annexing a bit of land whenever they can. Until his death in 1909, Ulsterman Sam McCaughey owned the world's largest farm, covering over one and a half million hectares (bigger than all of Northern Ireland) in Australia's Northern Territory.

- The Mourne region, which was made world-famous in a song by Percy French, was designated an Area of Outstanding Beauty in 1986.
- Percy (1854–1920) was neither French, nor a Northerner but from Cloonyquin, County Roscommon.
- There are no gay Orangemen, apparently.

Best Place To Survive
A Nuclear Attack

During the 1970s beautiful West Cork was invaded by hordes of hippies who believed it to be the safest, habitable place on earth to survive an H-bomb holocaust. Word had gone out on the hippy wire that **Ballydehob** and its ideal latitudinal/longitudinal coordinates (51 33 45 N and 9 28 38 W) rendered it immune to fall-out-carrying winds, and very quickly the locals were outnumbered in their own town by joint-toting Germans, Dutch and English drop-outs.

Little did these former marketing execs and ex-members of the Jimi Hendrix Experience (bass player Noel Redding moved here too) know that Ireland was targeted from all directions during the Cold War and was quite a dangerous place to be hanging out. In fact, there were several nukes pointed at Killybegs in County Donegal – the most westerly deep sea port in Europe – and at Monsignor Horan's Knock Airport in County

Mayo, which was built to the exact landing requirements of a B52 bomber.

There is also an unsubstantiated tale from 1976 of the Royal Navy removing a **Russian nuclear submarine** from Cork Harbour, which is considered to be one of the finest natural harbours in the world and a fantastic staging post for an attack on Britain[6].

None of this registered with West Cork's new inhabitants who were too busy harvesting and smoking their cannabis crops in the fields of that wild land. They got a bit of a jolt in 1978, however, when the Government decided to build the country's first nuclear power plant a few counties away in Wexford at **Carnsore Point**. So much for the Russians, the Paddys now wanted to nuke them.

After the Oil Crisis of 1973 the Dáil – and specifically George Colley and Dessie O'Malley – gave renewed effort to plans drawn up in 1968 which envisaged one, and eventually four, nuclear power stations to provide electricity for the entire country. The hippies of Cork were having none of it and swung (well, shambled) into action deploying the biggest weapon in their arsenal – the power of song. Joined by the two Chrises – **Moore** and **de Burgh** – and long-hairs from all over the world they invaded Wexford and organised a series of free concerts at Carnsore Point in 1978 and 1979 under the puntastic titles of 'Get To The Point' and 'Back To The Point' respectively. The shows such a success that public opinion was inflamed and the nuclear plans were shelved.

In fact the hippies did such a good job that Carnsore

---

[6] So much so that Churchill didn't want to give it up during the Treaty negotiations and the British held onto it and all Irish waters until 1938.

Point ultimately became the site of Ireland's first wind generating station, run by a subsidiary of the ESB.

After this the hippies returned to Cork and settled down to a life of making lentil sausages, hash marmalade and multi-coloured knitted hats out of ladies' armpit hair. One even translated Nena's '99 Red Balloons' into Irish.

After this the hippies returned to Cork and settled down to a life of making lentil sausages, hash marmalade and multi-coloured knitted hats out of ladies' armpit hair.

Imagine their horror if they'd known that just down the road University College Cork were storing 2.5 tonnes of **uranium** and a so-called 'student training reactor'. In 1980 Energy Minister George Colley told Leinster House that 'the sub-critical device' was 'acquired by University College, Cork, under a grant provided by the Government of the United States of America'. He was also asked to state 'the country and area of origin of the uranium which, according to one of the college's professors is held in the college for use in the nuclear device'. He declined on the grounds that such matters are confidential but informed the house that it was misleading to refer to the device as a reactor. It was, in fact, a 'sub-critical assembly of nuclear material in which the self-sustaining fission chain reaction cannot be established and maintained'. No, he probably didn't understand what he was saying either. In any event, he assured everyone that as the device wasn't a reactor, an emergency evacuation plan was not relevant.

'Nobody panic', in other words.

But what about the 2.5 tonnes of uranium?

As recently as July 2003, Green Party MEP **Nuala Ahern** was demanding to know why UCC was storing so much uranium on the campus. She also asked who was going to foot the bill – estimated to run into several million euro – for transportation of the material, and called on the government to outline what action it would take to remove the uranium from Cork.

A busy university campus might not be the ideal storage place for so much toxic material, but according to the Dáil reports of 1980 UCC was being monitored by the International Atomic Energy Agency and the Nuclear Energy Board and was about as safe as it could possibly be.

So the hippies were nearly right. The best place to survive a nuclear attack is Cork – in the Uranium Storage Unit in UCC.

INTERESTING FACTS

- In 2000, fans of English singer Robbie Williams were delighted to hear that the cheeky chappy was about to make his movie debut ... as a down-and-out hippie called Dylan in a comedy set in West Cork. The film, *Far From the Mushroom Cloud*, was to feature a group of hippies who travel to Ireland in 1978 believing the area to be safe in the event of a nuclear war. Both hippies and locals were to eventually unite in opposition to plans to build a nuclear power station. At the time of writing, the movie still hasn't seen the light of day.

- Ireland is sandwiched between Iraq and Israel in the world atlas. Between Iraq and a Hebrew place, as the saying goes. And there is an area in Kilkenny called Hebron. So much for the safe haven image.

Best Place To Survive An Earthquake

Inis Mór in the Aran Islands. Popular wisdom has it that Ireland is no great shakes when it comes to natural disasters. This green and pleasant island is off limits to serious earthquakes, tornados, tidal waves etc, and we can all sleep soundly in the knowledge that we won't be wearing the house around our neck in the morning.

Let's dispel the tornado myth first. Since the early Middle Ages there have been tales of twisters wreaking havoc across Ireland and our nearest neighbour. The phrase 'raining cats and dogs' dates from the medieval period and refers to household pets being sucked up into the vortex and flung across the countryside. Every year dozens of tornados are reported in Ireland and many more in remote areas go unrecorded. On New Year's Day 2005, a 'mini-tornado' damaged around 100 houses in **Clonee, County Meath**. The sudden storm ripped slates from roofs, smashed windows and overturned cars at around 1 pm. Locals reported feeling their houses shake and thought they were being struck by an earthquake. The fire service also responded to dozens of calls about structural damage in Counties Dublin, Kildare and Louth. There were 128 km winds at Dublin Airport, which caused two parked planes to collide. Miraculously nobody was injured.

Three years earlier on 21 March 2002 the BBC reported that **County Tyrone** had been caught in the path of a tornado. Windows were broken, cars crashed into each other, roof slates and debris flew through the air. The worrying thing is that incidents like these, although perfectly normal, appear to be on the increase, possibly due to climate change. And whereas the human race believes that by reducing carbon emissions we might actually slow down global warming and the occurrence of tornados, there is nothing we can do stop the earthquakes that are occasionally inflicted on Ireland by Mother Nature.

Earthquake Magnitudes

Minor	Less than 4	'D'you hear that?'
Light	4 to 4.9	'These Rice Crispies sure pack a punch.'
Moderate	5 to 5.9	'Go see if Mary Harney's fallen down the stairs.'
Strong	6 to 6.9	'There goes the neighbourhood.'
Major	7 to 7.9	'Aggggghhhhhhhhhhhhhhhhh!!!!!!!!'
Great	8 or more	*Silence.* (You're dead.)

One of the first reports of seismic activity in this region can be found in the *Annales Cambriae* (*Annals of Wales*).

The book refers to a great wind and an earthquake in the Isle of Man in 684AD and a tidal wave hitting Ireland in 720AD – as a result of an offshore quake. Exactly one year later the country was rocked again by a land-based shaker and again in 730AD.

One seventeenth-century writer, describing an earthquake felt in Dublin in 1534, remarked that 'they are such a rare thing in Ireland that when they happen they're considered a novelty'. They are not such a novelty across the water, however, and **Caernarvon** in Wales is the most seismically active area in Britain. Large and small earthquakes, usually accompanied by plenty of aftershocks, occur there at regular intervals and are felt in Ireland.

The last recorded large-scale event emanating from Wales happened on the morning of 19 July 1984, measured 5.4 on the Richter scale and had its epicentre on the Lleyn Peninsula. Although big, the focus of the quake was deep underground and so structural damage was limited. Nonetheless it managed to shake houses along our eastern shoreline. Two other recent earthquakes have occurred in the same area, in 1994 (magnitude 2.9) and 1999 (magnitude 3.2). This quake 'cluster' is located along the **Menai Straits** fault zone, a structure that runs across the Irish Sea, passing south of Carnsore Point. The fault dates back to the 'building' of Ireland and Britain 500 million years ago.

More recently an earthquake (magnitude 2.8) was recorded in the Irish Sea off Bray Head at 3.30 am on 14 December 2005. The 53 00 N 05 64 W epicentre was in an area not too far from a magnitude of 3.7 event recorded in 1951.

With all this seismic activity going on, the east coast is not the safest place to live if you want to survive an earthquake. Neither is the south coast according to Sir Charles Lyell's account of the aftermath of the great Lisbon earthquake of 1 November 1755: 'A great wave swept over the coast of Spain, and is said to have been 60 feet (18 metres) at Cadiz. At Tangier, in Africa, it rose and fell 18 times on the coast. At Funchal, in Madeira, it rose a full 15 feet (4.5 metres) above the high-water mark. At **Kinsale**, on the south coast of Ireland, a body of water rushed into the harbour, whirled round several vessels, and poured into the market-place.'

The north of Ireland isn't much safer as a place to live either. Rocks exposed on the shore at **Larne, County Antrim**, show that the area was shaken by an earthquake and a massive tidal wave 200 millon years ago. In fact many scientists believe that this is rock-solid evidence that the planet was struck by a giant meteorite – possibly the one that killed off the dinosaurs (who unfortunately later returned and took up politics in the Northern Ireland Assembly).

So where then is the Best Place To Survive an Earthquake? Based on the theory that nobody in their right minds wants to live in the midlands, the west coast has to be considered the only option. Galway is full of pseudo-'crusties' and stag parties so why not Inis Mór? It's unspoilt, boasts nice beaches, the people are friendly, and there's plenty of fish. More importantly, it's an island and if the prophecy of **St Columbcille** (520–597 AD)

Prosperous Ireland? Inundations? Seven years? Better pack your wellies, just in case.

comes to pass you'd be better off living anywhere other than on the mainland. The venerable cleric and founder of Iona off the west coast of Scotland concluded one of his prophesies with the following promise:

This new Éire shall be Éire the Prosperous; great shall be her renown and her power, and there shall not be on the surface of the wide earth a country found to be equal to this fine country. Seven years before the last day, the sea shall submerge Éire by one inundation.

Prosperous Ireland? Inundations? Seven years? Better pack your wellies, just in case.

INTERESTING FACT

- St Columbcille's prophecy could be coming true as you read this page – on the other side of the world. The island of New Ireland in the Papua New Guinea group is constantly being battered by huge quakes. The last one hit the island on 9 September 2005 and measured 7.3 on the Richter scale. New Ireland, by the by, is part of the Bismarck Archipelago and for much of its 320 km length is less than 10 km across. Its highest mountain is Lambel (2,150 m) and its capital is Port Moresby. Despite its name, New Ireland was colonised by the Bosch in the nineteenth century and there are no Irish people living there. And you thought we were making it up.

Best Place To Plant Spuds If You Want Them To Catch On

County Cork. Sir Walter Raleigh, who 'discovered' tobacco and potatoes, and was named after a three-speed push bike, was the first man to plant potatoes in Ireland on his estate in **Youghal** in 1585. Perhaps if he hadn't the Irish would have stuck to bread as their main dietary staple and the Great Famine would never have happened. Don't get us started about the tobacco.

INTERESTING FACTS

- Munster plums are, in fact, potatoes.
- In some parts of rural Ireland it is considered lucky to sow potatoes on Good Friday. What else would you be doing with the pubs closed?

Best Place To Keep 900-Year-Old Cheese

In the bog – no, not the toilet, that would be disgusting. The *bog* bog, where country folk live. In May 1987 a 1,000-year-old cheese was found perfectly preserved in a turf bank at Ballinamuck, County Tipperary. Paddy Cassidy made the lucky discovery when out cutting turf with his young son Jim. At first they thought they'd found a lump of clay buried in the bank but on closer examination they discovered it was a great lump of fat weighing more than 50 kg. It was subsequently dated to around the eleventh century and, except for a hard crust on its surface, it appeared to be in a near perfect condition.

In August of that year the renowned food critic Helen Lucy Burke actually tried a morsel of it, describing it as rancid with an athlete's foot whang. The texture, she added, was granular and was not unlike a dried-out Wensleydale.

The Ballinamuck cheese might, in fact, have originally started its long life as butter. Bog Butter is frequently found in Irish peatlands where it was stored in antiquity to keep it fresh. A cheese weighing 12 kg was found at Drumley Bog, County Donegal in June 1943, and in May 1999 a 300-year-old specimen weighing 32 kg was uncovered at Poll na gCapaill, County Galway. This custom of burying butter in the bog dates back to the sixth century and is referred to in an account of Irish food written by a chap named Dinely in 1681. He describes how butter is 'layed up in wicker baskets, mixed with a sort of garlic and buried for some time in a bog to make a provision of high taste for Lent'. That it was a special type of butter made for certain occasions is one possible explanation for the practice. Placing butter in a bog for a long period of time would enhance the flavour and keep it as cool as possible, while the exclusion of air and the antiseptic qualities of the peat would hinder mould growth.

It may also have been buried for reasons of security. During the Tudor and Stuart eras the English adopted the policy of destroying all foodstuffs to induce famine among the Gaelic clans. Much of the precious butter that was hidden may never have been recovered as the concealer may have been killed or taken flight.

Whatever the reasons, the practice died out in the early nineteenth century, ironically the century of the Great Famine.

It wasn't just butter that was buried in bogs by our ancestors – they liked to bury people as well. Over 80 bog bodies have been discovered in Ireland since 1750. Just think about that when you're sitting in front of a nice turf fire this winter. That lovely peaty smell could actually be someone's body part burning in your hearth. Or their hair gel. Hair gel? Two of the most intriguing bog body finds in recent years were those of two murdered men in Meath and Offaly, one of whom had manicured nails and the other a form of hair gel. The chap with the nice nails was a lanky 1.9 m tall – **The Tallest Iron Age Body Ever Found** – and like his fellow bog man was probably wealthy, well-connected and died about 2,300 years ago. **Old Croghan Man** and **Clonycavan Man** met horrible ends. The former was stabbed through the chest (an attack he saw coming as there is a defensive injury on his arm) and then decapitated and his body cut in half. Clonycavan Man had his gelled-up head split open with an axe before he was disemboweled.

Whereas Old Croghan was a real giant, Clonycavan was quite short at 1.6 m tall and he may have attempted to give himself greater stature by wearing his hair up in a Mohican style using 900–year–old pine resin hair gel imported from France.

The preservative properties of the bog were so effective that even the men's fingerprints are still visible and their discovery prompted a murder inquiry by the Gardaí.

All of the above proves that if bogland is good enough to preserve bodies then it's definitely the Best Place to Keep Cheese.

INTERESTING FACTS

- Covering 1,036 sq km, the Bog of Allen is The Largest Peat Bog in the World.
- The discovery of an eighth–century AD Psalter (Book of Psalms) by a Tipperary turf-cutter in July 2006 may not prove to be Ireland's Dead Sea Scrolls as some are eager to describe it. However, it does prove that, like ourselves, our ancestors liked to take a good book to the bog.

Best Place To Get Abducted By Aliens

The casual visitor to Boyle could be forgiven for thinking that little happens in this historic County Roscommon town. There's the lovely old monastery, with the lovely old B&B in its lee. Then there's the quiet old-fashioned snugly pubs and the quiet hotel with the honest-to-God roast beef lunches and the cups of tea on draught. And, of course, there's the river coursing through it. And that's about it.

Boyle is a quiet, quaint, charming, respectable old garrison town where, even on a Saturday night, the streets are deserted. Wisely, it would seem, as there is always the real danger of being abducted by aliens in Boyle.

In September 1997 the *Sunday World* ran a story describing a mysterious crash in the Curlew Mountains north of the town in May of the previous year. Witnesses saw a large silver saucer plunge from the sky, clip some treetops on a hillside and crash in a lake. According to some accounts, several occupants of the craft survived the crash and were taken into custody by the Gardaí. (If the crash didn't kill them, then the shock of a meeting a hairy-eared country Garda should have done the trick.) A NATO task force then reportedly moved into the 'zone' and stayed there for several months. According to the theorists, civilians were prevented from going near the scene and the local authorities were instructed to keep their noses out of it.

Stories were rife at the time of big black cars and men in suits hiking up mucky boreens and army helicopter searchlights scything the night sky. It was all very *Close Encounters* and word spread across the internet that ET had rammed his spacecraft into the Irish countryside (probably while phoning home on the mobile).

So seriously was the story taken that a group of UFO researchers descended on Boyle to investigate. Although their findings at the site didn't amount to much, the talk they gave in one of the pubs on 'UFO and Alien Life Form (ALF) phenomena worldwide' got the locals so interested that they set up their own society, which eventually became the **UFO Society of Ireland**, with a Ms Betty Meyler as its President.

Without wanting to poke fun at anyone's beliefs etc, it's hard not to wonder what the first words between Ms Meyler and an alien would be, should their paths ever cross: 'You can call me Betty and Betty, when you call me, you can call me ALF' spring to mind.

Since the foundation of the society there have been dozens more sightings, and people, who were originally too afraid to come forward, have been relating their own tales of flashing lights hovering over the Ballymote Road etc. As a result of all this activity, Boyle is now considered to be the UFO capital of Europe and – therefore – the town where you're most likely to be abducted by aliens.

The town where you're most likely to be abducted by ILLEGAL aliens, however, is further south in West Cork.

Best Place To Get Kidnapped By Algerian Pirates

Whatever about Boyle, the best place in Irish history for being kidnapped and sold into the white slave trade is Baltimore, County Cork.

In June 1631 this small coastal village, situated 13 km

southwest of Skibbereen, was attacked by pirates who had sailed all the way from Algeria in North Africa. Two inhabitants were killed in the raid and over a hundred were captured and sold into slavery. As the pirates had a pilot from Dungarvan to guide them into the small harbour – and those kidnapped were English settlers – it's safe to say that the Sack of Baltimore was organised by disgruntled native Catholics.

Boasting a shipbuilding industry and an export trade in tin, slate and textiles, Baltimore was considered a great prize by Spanish and Turkish seadogs in the early 1600s. It was also famous for having the biggest Curry House in Ireland, which is where it gets its name from in old Gaelic (*Baile an Balti Mór*). The sacking by 'Algerine' and his African men was by far the worst attack, however, and inspired balladeer Thomas Davis to write the imaginatively titled 'The Sacking of Baltimore'.

After finally realising that the town was too vulnerable to privateers the English responded by seating an Irish Barony there. However, John Bull didn't keep the garrison supplied with enough gunpowder for its cannons and Baltimore continued to be pillaged by pirates from other lands.

Today Baltimore has a population of about 200, including the Chief of the O'Driscoll Clan. Many townspeople wear eye patches and greet each other in the street with a hearty 'arrr, me hearty'. Cutlasses are banned, but there are still reports of tourists being boarded in broad daylight.

INTERESTING FACTS

- On 20 May 1518, a group of merchants from Waterford rounded up some rough chaps and sailed up the Barrow, pirate-style, in boats and ships to attack the town of New Ross, County Wexford. The crews included Spaniards, French, Bretons and Irish. The defenders surrendered the town's silver mace and 45 kg of silver to save the area.

- The difference between a pirate and a privateer is that the former was a sea robber and the latter was employed by governments in the seventeenth and eighteenth centuries to plunder enemy ships.

- The 200-tonne Irish-built and Irish-manned cutter *Black Prince* was said to be the fastest pirate ship sailing across the Atlantic in the late eighteenth century. She was commissioned by John Nixon of Philadelphia, a grandson of Irish emigrant Richard Nixon of Wexford. It was John Nixon who first read the Declaration of Independence to the people of Philadelphia on 8 July 1776. Interesting that the name Richard Nixon should be connected to anything dodgy to do with water.

Best Demolition Job

Horatio, Lord Nelson, had stared down stony-faced at the good people of Dublin for 158 years before the IRA blew his head off in 1966. The landmark Pillar on O'Connell Street, with its 40 m-high statue was erected in 1808 by the Lord Lieutenant of Ireland to commemorate the English admiral and the Battle of Trafalgar in 1805. His decision was not a popular one and he had to over-rule Dublin City Council to get his way. The subsequent statue, which predated the one in London by 40 years was open to the public and provided spectacular views of the city. It was also a painful reminder of our colonial past, and a number of individuals with a republican bent decided it had to go.

At 2 am on 8 March 1966 – 50 years after the Easter Rising – O'Connell Street was rocked by a massive explosion and the top part of the pillar was blown to smithereens, leaving only an ugly stump in its place. Remarkably, despite the fact that setting off bombs in public places is an incredibly stupid and dangerous thing to do, nobody was injured. The only damage caused outside of the target area was to a car parked on the street.

While not applauding this action, it has to be said that the demo men achieved their purpose and Nelson received his sailing orders.

Worst Demolition Job

On 10 March 1966 the Defence Forces attempted to destroy the remaining part of Nelson's Pillar, having deemed it beyond restoration. The subsequent explosion by the Army Engineering Corps blew out most of the windows on O'Connell Street and caused far more damage than the original blast. It also caused more than a few red faces.

And if you think that's a good opportunity for making cheap gags about public erections, then read on . . .

Best Place To Get Loved Up If You're A GAA Fan

Consider the options: Nowlan Park – too echoey, with all that corrugated roofing. Semple Stadium – too 'Tipperaryish'. Pairc Uí Chaoimh – possibly, although it's heard plenty of moans in its time. (It is in Cork after all) So where then?

It has to be **Croke Park**, HQ of Cumann Lúthcleas Gael, where they invented testosterone and made stick-waving a public spectacle. In September 2002 a pair of student lovebirds decided that the holy turf of Croker hadn't seen enough real action and paid it a visit on the eve of the Clare/Kilkenny hurling final. The couple (let's call them 'Peter' and 'Jane' to protect their real identities) climbed over the Jones' Road gate and gained access to the legendary pitch. Whether the 'square ball' rule was put to the test or not is still a mystery but the pair dozed off and were woken at 2 am by a Garda on security duty at the venue. The mildly surprised – one imagines – member of the Force reported that Jane was in a 'state of undress' with Peter lying beside her at the time.

Utterly mortified, the desperate duo later pleaded guilty to trespass and were ordered to pay €500 to charity. To their relief, however, the DPP decided to withdraw charges and, after an argument over legal precedent, the lovers were allowed to fade out of sight and into GAA lore. Not until, of course, a gleeful media had had its way with them.

In hindsight, despite Jane's 'state of undress' the couple may simply have entered Croker early to get a good seat on Hill 16. Nobody actually accused them of 'finishing the leather to the back of the net', as they say in GAA circles. Maybe it was just a very hot night.

The same equivocation can't be applied to the pair of out-and-out skangers who attempted a very public display of 'the choo-choo train going into the tunnel' in July 2006.

Outstanding organ the *Evening Herald* reported that commuters on a crowded south-bound Dart were horrified to witness a couple attempting to have sex no fewer than three times at rush hour. The exhibitionists stripped in the aisle and first tried to get it together standing up, but the man couldn't maintain his balance. His inamorata, who had cast off her tracksuit bottoms to reveal a pair of milky-white buttocks and a tiny thong, kneeled down and gave him some 'encouragement'. After achieving the desired result she then sat on him and did the deed. Finally, oblivious to all, the pair gathered up their clothes and dismounted at Bray. According to one onlooker they were so relaxed it was as if they did it every

> . . . gives a whole new meaning to the phrase 'getting a dart all the way to Bray'.

other afternoon. In mitigation, they did respect Iarnród Éireann's no-smoking policy and it gives a whole new meaning to the phrase 'getting a dart all the way to Bray'.

Co-incidentally, the bonkers bonkers would have passed another landmark to Irish sporting prowess on their romantic train trip home – Lansdowne Road. Six months prior to their railway romp, the home of the Irish rugby and soccer concluded an historic deal with the GAA to play their games at . . . Croke Park.

Foreign activities on the pitch at Croker? Who would have thought we'd see the day?

Best Place To Roar Your Head Off

The loudest roar for an outdoor stadium crowd – a reading of 125.4 decibels – was recorded at Lansdowne Road during the Ireland v Scotland Triple Crown match on 7 February 1998. The love train had just rattled by.

Worst Place To Dig For The Ark Of The Covenant

The Biblical Ark of the Covenant is generally described as being the sacred container in which Moses placed the Ten Commandments given to him by God. Its chief function was to act as a communications conduit between Moses and The Lord and it was housed in the Holy of Holies in Solomon's Temple in Jerusalem. Its very existence bore witness to the bond between Yahweh and his Chosen People and it both protected and chastised the faithful. In the sixth Century this priceless artefact disappeared and many historians believe it was destroyed by the Babylonians during the Fall of Jerusalem – many, but not all. There is a widespread and deep-rooted belief that the Ark was borne away during the battle for the Holy City and hidden for safe keeping. It was hidden too well however, and for millennia there has been an abundance of fevered speculation as to its whereabouts. Some claim it lies buried beneath what is now the Muslim shrine of the Dome of the Rock in Jerusalem. Others say it was secreted away to Ethiopia via Egypt and currently resides in the The Ethiopian Orthodox Church in Axum. Indiana Jones believed it could be found in Tanis, Egypt – and he was right – but that was just a movie.

So with all these signs pointing to a Middle Eastern resting place, where else would you go searching for the lost Ark of The Covenant but in **County Meath**?

In 1899 a group calling themselves the British Israelites began 'excavating' the Hill of Tara in the quest to find the Ark, provoking a ferocious outcry from Ireland's cultural custodians, including WB Yeats and Maude Gonne.

Tara, in case you weren't paying attention in history class, was the ancient seat of power in Ireland. A sacred

4,500 year-old site where 142 High Kings were crowned on the hilltop that was believed to have a direct connection with the underworld. There are so many legends attached to Tara that it would be impossible to relate them all in this book. In a phrase: it's a very, very, very, very, very important place in terms of our heritage.

The British Israelites, on the other hand, had no links to Ireland's heritage as far as Yeats and the boys were concerned. The movement began in the late eighteenth century and had as its central belief the notion that some ancient British and Celtic peoples were direct descendants of the lost tribes of Israel, deported from Samaria by the Assyrians in the eighth century BC. Nutters? The crowd that began digging up Tara 100 years ago believed the place was actually named after the Torah – the book of Jewish Law – and that the name of the renowned Irish bard, Heber, was a derivation of 'Hebrew'. They were convinced that the prophet Jeremiah had fled to Meath with Pharaoh's daughter Scota (Scotia/Scotland) after the siege of Jerusalem, bringing with them the treasures of the Temple including the sceptre of King David and the Ark amongst other things. Hopefully he also brought an umbrella and a pair of wellies.

After securing permission from the hill's owner, Gustavus Briscoe, the British-Isaraelites set about digging into the **Rath of the Synods**, a ring fort between the Mound of the Hostages and the Banqueting Hall. Nationalist Ireland was enraged and Arthur Griffith wrote a letter to the *London Times* declaring that Tara was 'a living reminder of the former glory of an enslaved and half-debased nation'. Yeats and company then went on an all-out offensive and staged protests on the hill, despite being warned off at gunpoint. **Maud Gonne**, in typically incendiary fashion, lit a fire and defiantly warbled 'A Nation Once Again' to the dismay of the local constabulary.

With the help of the media, the warrior-poets forced the British Israelites to disperse like the Lost Tribes in 1902. They had done a lot of damage with their mad digging and one member of their team had even thrown a gold bracelet into the Boyne, just because it wasn't the Ark. They also neglected to take notes of what discoveries they had made, although it can be said with certainty that they didn't find the Ark. However, they are reported to have come across a hoard of fifteen third-century AD Roman coins, a couple of shallow bowls with handles on their underside and a ring big enough for a giant.

No one knows what joker planted the coins, but it was definitely a local pair by the names of Shirley and Cecil Ball who planted the teapot lids and the napkin ring.

One hundred years on and the protestors and would-be excavators were back at Tara. This time it was 'Artics from the Continent' rather than the Ark of the Covenant at the centre of the dispute. Plans by the government to build the M3 motorway through the Tara Skryne valley near the treasured hill were met with the sounds of jaws hitting the floor at home and abroad. The dismay is not universal, however.

An estimated 22,000 commuters drive into Dublin from Meath every day and it was estimated that the M3 from Clonee to Kells would cut travelling times by 20 minutes each way. This works out as a whole week per year and the locals were very much in favour of the new time-saving road.

Isn't it a touch ironic that the passage of time may ultimately lead to the destruction of an area that survived it so well, for so long?

INTERESTING FACT

- Legend has it that candidates for the job of High King had to drive their chariots towards two pillar stones positioned closely together and which opened only for the rightful king. You'd have wanted to be pretty high to believe that all right.

Best Place To Worship The Hindu Elephant God, Ganesh

If County Meath is the worst place to go searching for the Ark of the Covenant then County Wicklow is Nirvana for those wishing to commune with the Hindu elephant God, Ganesh.

Hidden deep in the heart of the Garden County is Europe's most unusual theme park, **Victoria's Way**.

Visitors to this nine-hectare 'Spiritual Sculpture Park' are offered self-renewal by becoming 'at one' with the inner harmony of nature and its deep and healing essence. (That's what it says on the website at any rate.) They can even get spiritually lost in the Feminine Philosophy Maze, which must be something to do with men being better map readers than women. However, what really sets the Roundwood estate apart are the 'magical sculptures' – all twenty of them, ranging in height from 1.7 m to 5 m. They include a giant forefinger, a Bell of Forgetfulness, a drowning ferryman in a pond and a 3 m tall 'Mr Cool, The Nirvana Man'. And, if you're one of those searchers of the Ark of the Covenant at Tara, you could be forgiven for believing that you'd stumbled across Noah's Ark as you cross the threshold of the 'Victoria na Gig Birth Canal'[7].

There are also nine statues of elephants up to 3 m tall ranging in weight from 1.5 to 5 tonnes. These – and no disrespect is intended – are no mere elephants. However, these are representations of Hindu deity Ganesh/Ganesha, also known as Ganapati or Lord of Hosts. Ganesh is one of the most venerated figures in the Hindu faith and is the master of intellect and wisdom. He is known as the Remover of Obstacles and is often represented as a four-armed, pot-bellied god (with the head of a one-tusked elephant) that rides on the back of his servant, Mooshika the mouse. He is also generally depicted sitting down, with one leg raised off the ground. However, in this singular exhibition Ganesh can be found dancing, reading, reclining, playing the flute and

[7] This 6 m wide, 2 m high gateway is flanked by two very foxy-looking figures and looks like a gaping vulva with a slippery snake on top of it.

– be the hokey – knocking out a tune on the uilleann pipes, with a shamrock in his hat.

The park is the brainchild of **Victor Langheld**, a German philanthropist who survived the bombing of Dresden as a child and later travelled to India to discover enlightenment. Blessed with a large sum of money from his dad in his back pocket, Victor decided to set up an art and philosophy park in Ireland and thus Victor/Victoria's Way was born. All the Ganesh sculptures – designed by Victor – were made in Mahabalipuram, Tamil Nadu, India and imported to Ireland.

Victor isn't the only person to import eastern mysticism to our southeast. If Judaism (see Tara, above) or Hinduism aren't your bag, then a quick trip across the border to County Wexford is in order, for it is here that one will find Ireland's only **Temple to Isis,** the Egyptian/Grecian goddess. The Fellowship of Isis was founded in 1976 by Lady Olivia Robertson and her brother the Rev. Lawrence Durdin–Robertson and his late wife, Pamela, at Huntington Castle in Clonegal. They believe that men have been messing up the world (aren't we always?) and that the time is right for Isis to restore harmony between mankind and nature.

The Robertsons' place of worship can be found in the castle basement and, according to Olivia's book, *The Call of Isis*, it is most definitely not a museum but a living, working temple. There are 26 shrines within, including an intriguing array of religious and artistic items from a St. Bridget's cross to an old broom. On passing through the Temple of Isis portico in the basement, the faithful can anoint themselves at the 4.6 m well in the Chapel of Bridget or pay their respects at the shrines of Libra, Scorpio and Sagittarius. Thereafter they can move on to the Adytum, the holy of holies, dedicated to Ishtar with its picture of Dana (the goddess, not the Eurovision singer) or the Treasury with its engravings and pictures of the goddess. There is even a Tibetan bell made from eleven metals.

Apart from unusual religious imagery and practices, County Wicklow and County Wexford have another thing in common; along with County Waterford they comprise the **Three W's** – the only counties to bear Viking names. They are: Wykynlo (Viking Loch), Waesfjord (Inlet of the Mudflats) and Vadrafjord (Water Ford).

Wicklow (Cill Mhantain), despite its heathen Viking past, is also one of only three counties in Ireland that contain the word 'church' in its Irish name – the other two are Kildare (Cill Dara or Church of the Oaks) and Kilkenny (Cill Chainnigh or Church of St Canice). 'Cill Mhantain' derives from 'the Chapel of St Manntach the Toothless One'. The unfortunate missionary got his monicker after the locals knocked his teeth out while he and St Patrick were trying to land near the south harbour of the town. Undeterred by those who said he had bitten off more than he could chew, he returned and ultimately converted the place to Christianity. The descendants of some of these early Bray-folk still knock each other's teeth out near the harbour of a Saturday night in his honour.

After all that hassle St Manntach endured introducing Jesus to the locals, one wonders what he would make of Wicklow today being the Best Place In Ireland To Worship the Hindu Elephant God, Ganesh.

INTERESTING FACTS

- The Robertson family and its offshoots have lived in Huntington Castle since 1625. Family lore suggests they may or may not be related to the legendary Scota, queen of the Scots and Noah's niece Cesair – that's Noah of the Flood Ark, by the way, the one that carried the animals and came to rest on the top of Mount Ararat. Curiously 'Mount Ararat' is almost an anagram of 'Mound at Tara', except its missing a 'd' and has an 'r' to spare. Could this be where the confusion came about over the idea that the Ark of the Covenant is buried near the Mound of The Hostages in Tara?

- The elephant is the symbol of the US Democratic party – the most revered Irish-American member of which was JFK. In 1963 John Fitzgerald Kennedy, whose great-grandfather hailed from County Wexford, became the first US President to visit Ireland while holding office. Whatever about worshipping Ganesh, he was a great man for the divine females – Marilyn Monroe, Ava Gardner etc.

Worst Place To Live If You Have A Weak Chest

Anywhere in the Republic of Ireland. According to a report read to the joint Committee on Health and Children in July 2004, Ireland has the highest death rate from respiratory disease in western Europe. This rate – one in five people – is nearly twice the European average, with pneumonia (40%) and cigarette-related illnesses (25%) being the worst killers. Only those models of dynamism – Kyrgyzstan, Kazakhstan and Turkmenistan – have death rates from lung disease which exceed those of the Republic of Ireland. Sobering, isn't it?

Along with heart disease and non-respiratory cancer, lung diseases are the third major cause of death, and account for the most common reason to visit a GP. It's also been estimated that respiratory illnesses cost the health service over €317m annually and are the most commonly reported long-term illnesses in young adults. Social inequalities were reported to cause a higher proportion of respiratory disease deaths than in any other organ system.

Thought those figures were bad? Let's get on to cancer. A survey in the *Irish Examiner* published in July 2006 found that Dubliners are most at risk from deadly disease than their country counterparts. Citizens of our fair capital are 10% more likely to develop cancer than the average person living anywhere else in Ireland. This compares to Clare people who are 20% less likely to get the disease than a Dubliner. The capital also topped the league for the highest number of new cases diagnosed. And lung cancer killed more smokers in Dublin than anywhere else nationwide.

Mind you, there was some good news. Survival rates for Dubliners with cancer are slightly better than for people in other parts of the country. But then, the capital does have the largest concentration of cancer services in the land. And if you're thinking of moving from Dublin to Clare to enjoy its low cancer statistics, remember it rains a lot more in the west. Wouldn't want to catch pneumonia, now would you?

INTERESTING FACT

- There are far more uplifting things to read about than lung disease and cancer. Let's move on.

Best Place For Christmas Dinner If You Are In A Hurry

This distinction goes to Cootehill, County Cavan, the home of one Mr Vincent Pilkington. On 17 November 1980 Vincent became the **Fastest Turkey Plucker** in the world when he stripped a 7.25 kg bird in 1 minute and 30 seconds – which is fast food in anybody's language. Vincent became something of a superstar in the poultry world after his extraordinary feat was televised by the national broadcaster. Yes, well, there wasn't much else to talk about in Cavan back in the 1980s.

The plucky Ulsterman officially defeathered his last turkey in Bailieboro in December 2005. The 57-year-old had intended to pluck off in 2004, but was persuaded to carry on by his friends. Again, Cavan isn't exactly coming down with celebrities. The dad-of-two had lost none of his amazing speed and told reporters that he could still handle an average of sixteen turkeys in an hour (much like the judges on RTÉ 'talent' show *You're A Star*).

Happily for Vincent – and the rest of the country – his retirement as a one-man processing plant means he no longer comes under the secondary heading of Cavan Man Most Likely To Catch Bird 'Flu.

> Vincent . . . no longer comes under the secondary heading of Cavan Man Most Likely To Catch Bird 'Flu.

At the time of Vincent's retirement, there was genuine concern about the arrival of Avian 'Flu in Ireland. The last time the country was faced with a threat of this magnitude was in the aftermath of the Twin Towers atrocity. After that it trembled at the prospect of **Osama Bin Laden** crashing a plane into Sellafield and contaminating the Emerald Isle with radioactive fallout. Nobody was too concerned about Wales, oddly enough.

Much to the nation's surprise, it emerged that the Government had a plan in place for such a contingency. This surprise quickly turned to dismay when it turned out that the said plan only involved the distribution of iodine tablets to Irish homesteads. As the distribution of candles for the Millennium celebrations had been such a disaster – thousands were returned to Post Offices as a result of the disparity of letter box sizes across the country – little faith was placed in the assertions of Joe Jacob (FF), Minister for Nuclear War, that we'd all be 'grand'.

Then it was discovered that there weren't enough tablets to go around, resulting in Woodies and B&Q experiencing a rush on Extra Large Laminated White Tables under which the public could safely hide in the event of an Osama Meltdown.

At the time of writing, there are still no reasonable measures in place to deal with such a threat, unlike the plans drawn up for a Hitchcockian invasion of sick birdies.

In October 2006 the Government announced that it intends to deploy the army to draw a large tarpaulin – using poo-proofed articulated lorries – from Kinsale to the border in the event of even one bird being heard to sneeze in Irish airspace.

Meanwhile, as Vincent Pilkington is no longer a threat to the health of our nation, the State's G-Men have now turned their attention to Willy and Kitty Costello of Tuam. In November 1999 a 'White Peking' owned by the Galway couple laid the world's largest duck egg, measuring 14 cm in height, with a circumference of 20 cm, and weighing 227 g. There is no suggestion that the Costellos have any intention of breeding a race of super ducks, infecting them with 'flu and taking over the world. But you never know with Galway people.

INTERESTING FACT

- The World Record for Fastest Re-pluming of a Bird was set by Bosco Fogarty of Dalkey in January 2004. Mr Fogarty took 3 hrs 23 mins to re-feather a 3.2 kg chicken using Blu Tack and Evostick, between bouts of unconsciousness (his, not the bird's). He was not, as reported in the *Evening Herald*, 'sectioned' after causing the Second Bird 'Flu Scare Of Sandycove in the summer of 2005.

Best Place For Transatlantic Flight Records

The County of Galway holds this unique distinction in both the manned and unmanned categories.

Any aviation enthusiast worth his wings knows how **Alcock and Brown** were the first men to fly across the Atlantic from Newfoundland to the hinterlands of Clifden in 1919. Most people have been, hitherto fore, unaware that another trio of intrepid airmen, Maynard Hill, Barrett Foster and David Brown (all Yanks) also set a transatlantic flight record in Galway on August 11, 2003. On this occasion however, the pilots were not in the plane as it broke the record for Longest Distance Flight by a Model Aircraft. The lads radio-controlled the piston-engined 'The Spirit of Butts' Farm' 3,030 km from Cape Spear in Newfoundland to Mannin Beach, Galway without refuelling or landing. It was also the longest duration flight by a model aircraft, lasting 38 hours, 52 minutes and 19 seconds.

This was well over twice the time it took their predecessors to make the journey. Apart from this the only other major distinction between the trio and the boys of 1919 is that 'Alcock and Brown' sounds like a gay porno mag, while 'Maynard, Hill and Brown' does not.

Best Place To Be An Author

Dublin. Forget about James Joyce and all those other whingers complaining about not being recognised in their own country. Irish artists now enjoy limited tax free status (for the moment at any rate) thanks to the late **CJ Haughey** and his Artists' Tax Exemption Scheme of 1969. This was designed to encourage writers and musicians to stay in the Ould Sod and 'give us a bar or two' or 'tell us an ould story there', as CJ might have put it. OK he didn't put it quite like that, but it worked and top musos, loads of really crap poets and chick lit authors stay put instead of inflicting themselves on the rest of the world. Most Irish authors now live in the Greater Dublin Area where they're within shouting distance of the latest photo opportunity, while the rest are living in parts of Kerry.

The other side of this tax-free 'pingin' was that with **Bono** and **Neil Jordan** and **Van the Man** staying and buying up houses all over the place, prices went through the roof, especially in Dalkey, and soon people were spending mad amounts of money on 'bijou homes'.

The other reason Dublin is the best place to be an author is because it also has the richest literary prize in the world – The international **IMPAC Dublin Literary Award**. This was started in 1996 and has a rather sweet pot of €100,000 for single works of a 'high literary merit'. According to its website[8] the award is the 'largest and most international prize of its kind. It involves libraries from all corners of the globe, and is open to books written in any language'.

The writer of the preceding sentence will never win the IMPAC, but is this year's recipient of the **Erindipity Award for Using a Redundant Cliché**. Globes don't have corners.

INTERESTING FACT

- In June 2006 Colm Toibín became the first Irish author to win the IMPAC prize for his book, *The Master*. Despite being a Wexford man, Colm resides in the capital, which proves that Dublin is definitely the best place to live if you're an author and want to win a load of money.

Best Biscuits For Irish Dancers

As Hibernian as Mariettas and Fig Rolls undoubtedly are, the bicky of choice among top Irish dancers is the

[8] www.impacdublinaward/index.htm

mighty Jaffa Cake. Or at least for Michael Flatley at any rate. A *Times* reporter noted during a backstage interview in November 2005 that the Lord of The Dance had boxes of them stacked on a table in his dressing room. The explanation was that the Super Hoofer eats the spongy, chocolatey treats with the orangey centre for energy before shows. A single Jaffa Cake is a high-kicking 46 calories but has only a low, low, limbo-dancing 1g of fat. This is why Michael Flatley is not Michael Fatley, or so they say.

Some suspect he also might roll around in Jaffa Cakes instead of using fake tan. This would explain why his face sometimes looks like one with the chocolate licked off.

Best Place To Paint Your Castle Pink And Not Get Beaten Up

County Cork is the safest place to paint your castle a pastel shade and not get run out of town or 'bashed' coming home from the pub at night. British movie star Jeremy Irons proved this when he decided to choose a rather camp peach/pink colour for his rugged fifteenth-century dream home, Kilcoe Castle, near Ballydehob.

The crushed-satin-voiced Jeremy, who is renowned for wearing yellow jump suits and Rasputin fur ensembles, paid €3.2 m for the crumbling tower house in the late 1990s with his wife, **Sinéad Cusack**, and invested a huge amount of time, effort and money in getting everything 'just so' (as they say in the theatrical world).

Kilcoe had originally been covered with a thick coat of

'render', patches of which still clung to the building. The medieval builders, realising the castle's stonework would never be a match for the weather – as the house was so close to the head of the bay – protected it with a mixture of clay, sand, lime and gravel. This in turn was covered with coats of white limewash and, in some places, ketchup from their jumbo breakfast rolls.

Jeremy later wrote in *The Irish Times* that despite his desire to return the castle to its original external condition, he had a soft spot for the naked stonework displayed at Kilcoe. He hoped that by painstakingly pointing the joints he could make the tower both watertight and a site for sore eyes.

Picture then, pastel-boiler-suited Jeremy and his eleven co-workers, spatulas in hand, filling the smallest flaws in the stone and then scrubbing down the castle with acid to remove any trace of lime over a period of nine months, in all weathers. No sooner did the scaffolds come down than the winter storms arrived and the castle leaked like an octogenarian's underpants. And so it was back to the drawing board, or Jeremy Iron-ing board, for the Hollywood heartthrob. In the end, he decided that rendering – the less attractive option – would be the solution. This protective layer would, in theory, then be covered with ten coats of white limewash – a colour the couple felt was too stark for the surrounding area. After fretting and experimenting, and fretting some more, Jeremy and Sinéad landed on the perfect colour to compliment the verdant fields, chameleon bay and the swirling palette of the Munster sky – pink. This was achieved – for those of you with a scientific bent – by adding Copperass, or ferrous sulphate, to the wash.

Following its completion after 35 months of hard labour in 2001, Cork County Council declared itself happy with the paint-job and no one has since questioned Jeremy's manliness for living in a Pink Castle. After all he was a very convincing bad guy in *Die Hard with a Vengeance* (1995).

INTERESTING FACTS

- Jeremy is not planning to make a movie called *Dye Pink with Abandon (2007)*, co-starring Bruce Willis, about two out-of-control interior designers.
- The Irons family restored part of Ireland's heritage without any grants or tax breaks.
- Sinéad's legendary father, the much-loved Cyril Cusack, took a London audience by storm with his portrayal of Christy Mahon in JM Synge's *The Playboy of The Western World* at the Haymarket in 1943. Unfortunately, the play he was supposed to be appearing in was *The Doctor's Dilemma* by GB Shaw. Laurence Olivier was not amused, had him booted out of the Old Vic Theatre Company and Cusack didn't work in London for another 20 years. His 'mishap' was later blamed on being served 'bad booze'.

Another great man for the Cork castles and a dash of colour is Michael Flatley. The dancer – who looks like a man who washes in Lucozade – spent an estimated €40m renovating Castlehyde House, Fermoy, in County Cork. The building is regarded as one of the finest examples of Georgian architecture in the southwest and boasts 14 bedrooms, a 20-seat private cinema, a (health) spa, two climate-controlled wine cellars and a three-storey library.

Unlike Jeremy Irons, Flatley stopped short of painting his home pink, although if he had, there are few on Cork County Council who would have asked him to 'step outside'. Flatley, who started dancing with his granny in Chicago when he was four, took his first proper Irish Dance Classes in Chicago at the age of eleven. While the body oil and leather jerkins were a long way off, the jiggery pokery was bound to attract the attentions of the bigger boys on the block and, sensibly, Michael was sent to boxing school. Ever the high-achiever, young Mike went on to win the Chicago Golden Gloves Amateur Boxing Championship. So even if he decided to stick a flamingo on his head and paint his entire 60-hectare estate Sunset Blush, no one in their right mind was going to argue with him. Or so you would think.

In fact Flatley, who is worth an estimated €375m and whose legs are insured for €40m, had endless trouble keeping the planners happy. At one point, fed up with all the red tape, he halted renovations at the 1801-built castle on the Blackwater after being refused permission for a gym and two decorative ponds.

Now whatever one might say about men who like to work up a good sweat before tending to their water features, no one could ever accuse the former builder of being a touch 'pink'. Despite his choice of work clothes – tight pants, headbands, Uncle Sam suits and make-up – Flatley has had a phenomenal ability to pull the opposite sex and, in his prime, has dated some of the world's foxiest mamas. Besides, he likes his pints.

The mayor of Fermoy told the *Irish Examiner* during the pond crisis that Flatley was the best ambassador the town ever had, citing his donations to the community hospital and – more importantly – his visits to local pubs.

So, it would appear that Cork may be the Best Place To Paint Your Castle Pink, but not to install a nice manly gym, even if you like to paint the town red once in a while. However all-dancing, all-boxing, pint-drinking bazzilionaire Flatley may have his own way in the end. The unofficial ambassador of Fermoy, whose Castlehyde pile is the ancestral home of President Douglas Hyde, has hinted that he wants a crack at the Áras himself.

If he succeeds, the future may not be so rosy for Cork's planners.

INTERESTING FACTS

- The last recorded duel fought in County Cork took place in Castlehyde in 1832.

- Michael Flatley is the fastest tap dancer in the world, recording a phenomenal speed of 35 taps per second in 1998 at the age of 39.
- Flatley also works his way through 100 pairs of dance shoes a year. Think 'Imelda Marcos with rhythm'.

Staying with the colour theme, castle-owner **Chris de Burgh's** favourite one is neither golden tan nor pink, but red. When he's not acting the goat with the Nanny, the pint-sized singer/songwriter likes to sing the praises of his beautiful wife, Diane. Red was also the colour of Chris' face when it became public knowledge that he had been playing offside on his aforementioned wife. But that's all in the past and we're not going to rake over those old coals (you can still 'Google' him if you're that desperate).

Chris is the proud owner of twelfth-century Bargy Castle, County Wexford, which was bought in 1960 by his British diplomat dad, Charles Davison, and his Irish secretary mum, Maeve Emily de Burgh. After they renovated the place it was opened up as a half-year holiday hotel. The young Chris did his first concerts in this castle and he used to sing for the guests in the evenings before going on to study English and French at Trinity College Dublin. Considering the lyrics to 'Lady in Red' are hardly challenging, this might seem like time wasted. However, even the most avowed detester of that song will grudgingly admit that his good material – 'Spanish Train and Other Stories' for example – outweighs his bad.

Whatever about him singing in it, there's been more than a few screeches heard to emanate from Bargy Castle over the centuries. The most ill-fated of Bargy's owners was **Beauchamp Bagenal Harvey**, a lawyer and member of the United Irishmen. At the age of 36, he was in command at the disastrous battle of New Ross on 5 June 1798. That defeat, and the savage massacre of over 100 suspected loyalists at Scullabogue on the same day, left him a broken man. Two days later he was replaced as Commander-in-Chief and planned an escape to France, but like many others he was betrayed and hanged. It is a moot point whether the same should be done to Chris for writing 'Lady in Red' and the execrable 'Blue Jeans'.

With the castle's republican history, Chris would be perfectly entitled to paint it green, white and orange. However, he would also be within his rights to daub it sky blue and white, with a smiley May sun in the middle – the colour of the Argentinian flag.

For Chris J de Burgh Davison is only a plastic Paddy (he's also a Libran, but that's irrelevant). Ireland's most successful romantic warbler/writer is actually Argentinian and only moved here when he was 12 years old.

What next? The revelation that half of Irish supergroup U2 are British and that only one of them is a good baptised Catholic? Happily, Chris has no plans to repaint his home but if he ever did, he might consider renaming the place Argy Bargy Castle.

INTERESTING FACTS

- Dave Howell Evans (Edge) was born on 8 August 1961 in Barking, East London. Adam Clayton was born on 13 March 1960 in Chinnor, Oxford and Larry Mullen Jnr was born on 31 October 1961 and was baptised in Artane, County Dublin.

- Chris got his break in 1974 when he was discovered singing in Captain America's on Grafton Street, Dublin. Whether or not it was in exchange for food is not on record.

- Chris is a fan of the Cottage Pie in Finnegan's of Dalkey, County Dublin.

- 'Lady in Red' has sold 8 million copies worldwide.

- If Chris de Burgh was really Irish his name would be Christy Burke.

And finally **Enya**, the last of the colourful artist/castle owners. This raven-haired Ulster beauty bought 160-year-old Ayesha Castle on Victoria Road in Killiney, County Dublin for IR£2.7m (€3.4m) in September 1997 and then spent the next five years doing it up. Set in 1.4 hectares of wooded grounds the romantic castle is surrounded by a tall granite wall and sits high on a south-facing slope looking out over Killiney Bay. The estate boasts three reception rooms and six bedrooms in the main building, with two separate apartments overlooking a central courtyard and an art gallery with a separate entrance. Following its refurbishment Enya renamed the fairytale mansion 'Manderley' after the house in her favourite movie *Rebecca* (1940), based on the Daphne du Maurier novel. Being shy and rich in equal measure (she was the joint 78th richest person in Ireland in 2005 with an estimated €100m) she could easily afford the €250,000 spent on privacy measures for her new home.

Proving that money can't always buy you security, the castle had two serious breaches in Autumn 2005, the second being particularly frightening for the swirly-voiced singer. On 5 August a stalker broke into Manderley and reportedly tied up a maid, then spent two hours looking for Enya, who was hiding in a panic room. The intruder finally bolted with a number of items when the terrified Donegal woman activated an alarm. Only one week earlier another 'visitor' was caught in the grounds attempting to gain access to the castle.

This was not the first time that Enya had suffered at the hands of stalkers. In 1996, a 31-year-old Italian, who had moved to Dublin to be near her, stabbed himself outside her family's pub in Gweedore in County Donegal. Is it any wonder that the poor woman, who was the world's biggest-selling artist in 2001, has a reputation for closely guarding her privacy?

Despite the prevailing image of her hiding away in a turret, Enya insists she is not a recluse and likes to have friends around and do the things normal folk like to do.

Well, even Rapunzel let her hair down once in a while.

If the Donegal Diva ever decides to paint her castle, she might consider a nice green and brown camouflage job to confuse the fruitcakes.

INTERESTING FACTS

- Nobody knows what Enya's favourite colour is as she's always shrouded in mist.
- Eithne Brennan was first credited as Enya for writing some of the music for the 1984 movie *The Frog Prince*.
- Kilkea Castle, County Kildare is the oldest continuously inhabited castle in Ireland. It was built in 1180 by Sir Walter de Riddlesford, a young knight who had accompanied the first invasion party of Anglo-Normans in 1170.

Most and Least

Most Money For A Beach Hut

The year 2006 finally proved beyond a reasonable doubt that Ireland is Europe's largest open-air nuthouse. **Neptune Cottage** in Kilcoole, County Wicklow was put on the market and almost immediately had three offers on the table. And, actually, to read the brochure description the beach pad doesn't sound half bad: sea on your doorstep . . . unrivalled location . . . mature enclosed garden . . . chemical outdoor toilet . . . mains water and electricity nearby.

As we said, not half bad if you're talking about the first half of that sentence. Neptune Cottage is a two-room, 18.5 sq m, electricity-free, timber hut on 670 sq m site, dating from 1936, which probably makes it a period residence. It also backs onto the Dublin/Rosslare railway line, the noise of which should take its owners' minds off the howling sea storms during the winter months as they warm themselves beside the bottle-gas stove.

The asking price? A bargain at €120,000 – the most money offered for a beach hut in the history of the state. Prior to this the most money ever paid for a seafront property was €7.5m when 1 Sorrento Terrace in star-spangled Dalkey went on the market in 1998.

Still, the beach hut has its plus points over Sorrento Road. Residents there, including Neil Jordan, wake each morning not only to a view of the sea, but also to the sight of former Formula 1 lothario Eddie Jordan's monstrous erection.

The towering four-storey 'home' can be seen from Bray on a clear day.

Most Popular Seaside Resort (With Dubliners)

The Northies have Royal Portrush and Bundoran, the Westies have Rosses Point and The Rocks of Connacht, and the Southies have Spike Island – but Dubliners will always have **Courtown**. Voted The World's Best Resort Ever in Ireland twelve times from 1986 to 2006 (there was an outbreak of badgers in 2005) this little Wexford town is the Cannes of the sunny southeast. Boasting long sandy beaches and record levels of skin blistering sunshine, even after dark, Courtown has been welcoming tourists since 1278 when the first chip shop – or Magasin du Pommes Frites as the Normans called it – opened near the old harbour. And those tourists keep coming back for more.

(Not the original ones from 1278, obviously. They're all dead. New ones.) And why wouldn't they, as there's something to suit everyone's taste in fabulous Courtown.

Hungry? No need to wait months for a table at snooty old La Villa des Lys or La Palme d'Or – just pull on your cleanest shellsuit and queue for a one-and-one like everybody else in one of the many fine food emporia. Then dine al fresco, dodging the seagulls and wasps while small children fling poo at you using their buckets and spades. Follow that with a stroll along the beach with a bottle of Blunden Village Super Strong Extra Knacker Cider before passing out on a sand dune with your trousers around your ankles and nettle rash around your unmentionables. Superbe.

Fancy a flutter, but too bored with passé Monaco to go and break the bank at Monte Carlo? Sober up and head down to the arcades and make a bundle out of the week's Mickey Money[9] on the slots or try your skill on the video games. Besides it's a good way to stay out of the southeast's renowned midday furnace.

Shopaholic? Cartier, Gucci, Emporio Armani, Boss, Longchamps are but a limo ride away. No stop, that's Cannes. The tourists of Courtown have no time for such crass shrines to conspicuous consumption. According to www.courtownharbour.com there are 'quite a number' of shops for ice creams, groceries and beach toys, not to mention the local garage, a beauty salon, a craft shop and a gift shop. Best of all, Courtown can boast that it is only 5 km away from the shopping Mecca of Gorey with its electrical shops, hardware shops and – stop flexing that

[9] Children's Allowance to you.

plastic – Tesco, Pettits, Lidl and Aldi.

Cannes, me bollix (as they say in the Fair City). This year, do like the Dubs do and go to Courtown. Or we'll come around to your house and burst you.

INTERESTING FACT

- The author has never been to Courtown.

Place Most Likely To Get A Puck In The Gob

Standing in the line of fire of hurling legend **Tom Murphy**, of Three Castles GAA club, County Kilkenny. Tom holds the record for the longest 'Lift and Stroke' puck of a sliothar – a mighty 118 m, which he set in 1906 (it was 129 yards back then). Obviously he doesn't play much any more (as he's dead), but if he did you'd want to keep your head down in the presence of such an incredibly strong individual with a big stick in his hand.

Former Cork goalkeeper **Ger Cunningham** is another mighty pucker having won the All-Ireland Puc Fada contest a record seven times. This 'Long Puck' contest is held annually in the Cooley Mountains in County Louth and is a great test of a hurler's playing skills. Twelve players compete each year over the 5 km course. Starting at Annaverna, they hit the ball up the side of Carn an Mhadaidh and back down to finish in Aghameen. The player with the lowest number of pucks wins. Think golf, but without the Pringle sweaters and with some serious hazards to negotiate.

The record 'Puck Strike' currently stands at 48 and is held by **Brendan Cummins of Tipperary**, a county with a proud tradition of producing top class hurlers. The greatest of these, in many people's opinion, is the dashing **Nicky English**, who scored the highest individual tally ever achieved in a Senior Hurling Final, 18 points (2-12) against Antrim in 1989. Nicky's other talent was bleeding. Eschewing the restrictiveness of a helmet, this magical player was forever attracting hurleys onto his head and generally getting brutally treated by the opposition. This was good for his team-mates, however, as the opposing team were generally so busy trying to mark Nicky out of the game that they didn't have time to rough up anyone else.

Because of this, being on the same team as Nicky English was a good place to be if you didn't want to get a puck in the gob.

INTERESTING FACTS

- The GAA is the largest sporting organisation in Ireland. It has 2,800 clubs, 97,000 hurlers, 182,000 bogballers and 800,000 members at home and abroad.

- The largest ever attendance at a Senior Hurling Final was 84,856, at Cork's victory over Wexford in 1954. The largest attendance ever in Croke Park was 90,556 in 1961 when Down played

Offaly in the football final. This attendance can never be equalled or bettered as the capacity of the venue has been reduced over the years to 79,500.

- Over 1,800 tonnes of steel were used in the construction of the roof for the new supersized Croke Park and the length of the steeped terracing is 42 km. (You might need to know that someday.)

- Puc Fada is not to be confused with Puck Fair, which is held in Killorglin, County Kerry every August. During the festival the locals crown a billy goat and call him King Puck. Speaking of billy goats' beards, there's also a Queen of the Muff Festival elected in Donegal during the same month.

Place Most Likely To Meet The Parish Pope

If you're thinking the Phoenix Park or Galway because of their associations with the visit of Pope John Paul II in 1979, think again. The place you're most likely to bump into the Parish Pope is **Kilfenora** in County Clare. This is because the bishop of that Diocese has been none other than Il Papa himself since 1866.

Like all things to do with religion in Ireland, it's kind

of complicated. The first monastic settlement in Kilfenora was founded by St Fachtna in the sixth century. After several centuries of political intrigue by the local clans it became a diocese in 1152 with its own bishop and cathedral.

The 'City of the Crosses', as Kilfenora became known, maintained its independence until 1750 when it was united with the Diocese of Kilmacdough across the border in County Galway. Ireland at this time was divided into four ecclesiastical provinces – Armagh, Dublin, Cashel and Tuam. As Kilfenora was in Cashel and Kilmacdough in Tuam they both had the right to keep their separate identities. To deal with the delicate issue of which bishop would be in charge of both dioceses, they settled on the idea of alternating government. This meant that the first bishop of the united dioceses was the Bishop of Kilmacdough and Apostolic Administrator of Kilfenora and his successor was the Bishop of Kilfenora and Apostolic Administrator of Kilmacdough and so on.

This arrangement lasted up until the retirement of the last Bishop of Kilmacdough, Patrick Fallon, in 1866. At this point the dioceses were united with the diocese of Galway, and the bishop of that burg was appointed Apostolic Administrator of Kilfenora by Papal Bull. Because the Bishop of Galway is technically administrating Kilfenora on behalf of the 'Big Guy' in Rome, it is, officially, the Pope's diocese. Therefore Il Papa is the Bishop (or Parish Pope) of Kilfenora.

The current Pope (Benedict) is not renowned for being a mad partyman, which is a shame, because as Absentee

Parish Pope of Kilfenora he's missing out on the town's world famous musical tradition and in particular, its world famous céilí band. **The Kilfenora Céilí Band** was born four years after Il Papa took over the reins in Clare in 1870. Back then it was a fife and drum outfit but changed instruments in 1908 when the parish priest (as opposed to Parish Pope) was trying to raise money to refurbish the church. Canon Cassidy organised fundraising dances in the schoolhouse with the musical group, and the Kilfenora Ceili Band never looked back.

The current Pope (Benedict) is not renowned for being a mad partyman, which is a shame, because as Absentee Parish Pope of Kilfenora he's missing out on the town's world famous musical tradition . . .

The shindigs were hugely popular with the locals although most people grumbled about how Canon Cassidy was very strict on any wild lepping or wheeling in the set. A little 'yahooing' was acceptable but Frenchying and dropping the lámh were definitely out. Mind you, it's not easy to drop the lámh on someone when they're dancing to 'The Walls of Limerick'. It's not known whether the practice of 'bushing', i.e. taking your knickers off before a dance and leaving them in a hedge, was as widespread as it is now. With the Pope hearing confessions locally, probably not.

Most Amazing Maze

The world's largest permanent hedge maze can be found at **Castlewellan** in County Down. The so-called 'Peace Maze' covers an area of 11,215 sq m and has a total path length of 3.5 km, which is a respectable stretch of the legs for any maze enthusiast. How someone could find wandering around a maze 'peaceful' is anyone's guess. 'Panic Maze' or 'HEEEELLLLLLLLLPPPPPP!!! I'm Lost Maze' or 'Get me a Large Strimmer Maze' might be more appropriate names.

This maze is not to be confused with the North's other famous Maze – **Long Kesh prison** – where 25,000 of Ulster's hardmen did a long stretch at some stage or other. HM Prison The Maze began its career as an RAF station at Long Kesh, 16 km outside of Belfast near Lisburn, and became the enduring symbol of the Troubles. Its darker history began in 1971 with the introduction of internment without trial. The British Intelligence raid 'Operation Demetrius' on the homes of 452 paramilitary suspects in August of that year yielded 342 republicans. However, the most important IRA figures had been tipped off and many of the detainees were allowed to go home when it became clear that they had no paramilitary connections. By 1972 there were 924 internees living in Nissen huts, separated by political affiliations. The prisoners demanded better conditions and in 1974 Special Category Status – de facto 'political status' – was introduced for 1,100 inmates. They now had the right to free association, wear their own clothes etc. As the conflict progressed and became even bloodier, this status was rescinded and in 1976 the British Government introduced a policy of criminalisation for any new prisoners entering the Maze. Those subsequently convicted of terrorist offences would be housed in eight H Blocks and the era of the dirty protest and the hunger strike was ushered in as the Republican inmates demanded political status.

In 1981 the first of two world headline-grabbing events came to pass at the Maze. The funeral of hunger striker **Bobby Sands**, leader of the IRA prisoners, drew 100,000 people on to the streets of Belfast. Sands, who had been elected to the Houses of Parliament in April, spent 66 days refusing food and passed away on 5 May. Another nine hunger strikers were to follow by the end of August as the new government of Margaret Thatcher stood firm.

Twenty-five years after the death of Bobby Sands, and six years after its closure, a new plan was unveiled to transform the derelict jail into a shining example of the North's transformation. The 146-hectare development is to include a 42,000-seater sports stadium, a multi-screen cinema, a high-end hotel, restaurants, an indoor equestrian centre and an international centre for conflict transformation. It might even have an ice rink.

Most of the blocks will be razed but the hospital wing where Sands died will be preserved. The project is aimed at regenerating the peacetime economy but, even after the publication of details in March 2006, there was more trouble and the final decision to build the £120m (€192m) complex was put on hold. This was to listen to lobby groups who protested that any new stadium should be built within Belfast and not 16 km down the road.

More importantly it was aimed at giving the three main sporting bodies – Soccer (IFA), Rugby (IRFU) and Gaelic Games (GAA) – time for negotiations to secure their commitment to sharing facilities. The Northies just love to talk.

The second major event at The Maze was the 1983 breakout when 38 prisoners flew the coop. It remains the biggest prison break in British history.

After that escapade, one imagines the World's Largest Permanent Maze at Castlewellan would be a doddle to those desperadoes.

INTERESTING FACT

- If the North's hedges were anything like the big ignorant ones down in Offaly then the Castlewellan Maze would actually be visible from space, like the Great Wall of China or Liberty Hall. This is because Birr Castle has the odd distinction of owning both the tallest and oldest box hedge in Ireland and The Biggest Telescope In The World. The box hedge is a strapping 11 m high and a venerable 300 years old. The telescope, built by the Earl of Rosse in the 1840s was the largest scope in the world for 70 years and made some remarkable discoveries about the make-up of galaxies. It has been estimated that if the telescope was trained on the box hedge (on a clear night) the latter would be visible from Uranus.

Most Amazing Flower

Mazes and box hedges aside, one of the greatest feats of green-fingering on this green and pleasant isle was performed by a Ms Lydia Foy from Athy, Co Kildare. Whereas it took Birr Castle's box bush three centuries to grow into the monster it is today, it took Ms Foy considerably less time to grow The World's Biggest Foxglove in her back garden in 1997. Her spectacular flower stood a towering 3.29 m.

If Ms Foy lived in Birr she could have claimed to have grown the world's biggest BIFFO (Big Ignorant Foxglove From Offaly). Unfortunately she doesn't and, on top of that, her record has since been broken by an 81-year-old English pensioner, who can boast of having a whopping 3.6 m specimen in his back garden. Interestingly, the 81-year-old gardener's name is Bill Leake.

Most Amazing . . . Horseradish?

Mr Leake and Ms Foy may be Triffid-Masters when it comes to growing sweet-scented garden flowers, but they're in the ha'penny place when compared to Jolly Green Giant, Harry Crowley.

Dubliner Harry will be best remembered for setting what is probably the least-attempted of all gardening records – Growing The Longest Horseradish In The World. Admittedly, the humble radish may not be as alluring as other members of the plant kingdom, but what Harry's pride and joy lacks in looks it makes up for in length. The fiery salad vegetable measures 2.5 m, three quarters of which comprise the root hair alone.

Walkinstown's 'A Man Called Horseradish' already holds national titles for growing the Longest Carrot, Longest Parsnip and Heaviest Potato in Ireland.

'Gardening is like studying radio or like studying electricity, which I have studied. It is colossal, and you have to know a lot of theory,' said the 62-year-old of his achievement, omitting to mention that nobody has ever been electrocuted by a garden vegetable.

Whether Harry subsequently plans to genetically modify a herd of Aberdeen Angus and grow the World's Biggest Yorkshire Pudding, is not on record.

INTERESTING FACTS

- Foxgloves normally grow to 1.5 m tall.
- No one has ever got permanently lost in the Peace Maze (that we know of).

Most Difficult Question To Answer If You're A Dubliner

In a straw poll on Grafton Street in May 1973, 85,000 Dubliners were asked the following question. No one could answer it.

Question: Name the five places in Dublin that end in an 'O'. Phibsboro is not one of them as it is an abbreviation of Phibsborough. Neither is Monto (Montgomery Street).

Here's a clue: some of them have a Latin feel to their names while one is so wild the inhabitants have been known to eat their young.

Answer: Rialto, Portobello, Marino, Pimlico. The last one is Dublin Zoo.

Most Square Of Dublin Squares

Mountjoy Square is the squarest of squares in the capital. In fact it's the only real square-shaped 'square'. All the rest are battered parallelograms and ruptured rhomboids and rectangles – Mountjoy Square is as long as it's wide at 55 sq m.

Least Square Of Dublin Squares

Fitzwilliam Square. Go there after dark if you don't believe us.

Most Mobile Part Of Ireland

Students of Irish geography will already know that the most northerly part of the island is in the South, as is the most westerly part, and the most easterly part is in the North.

However, it may come as a surprise to learn that the centre of Ireland has rambled all over the shop throughout antiquity – and there is still some debate as to its whereabouts. Before we get to this, let's get the opening sentence explained. The northernmost point in Ireland is near Malin Head on the Inishowen Peninsula in County

Donegal – which is officially in the South, i.e. the Republic. The westernmost point is Garraun Point on the Dingle Peninsula in the deep south of County Kerry, and the easternmost place is Burr Point in Northern Ireland's County Down. And finally the southernmost point is Brow Head in County Cork.

The reason for all this confusion is intertwined with Ireland's history as a favourite invasion or holiday destination for all manner of rude types: Vikings, English, Welsh, etc. According to **Blessed Bosco Fogarty** in his eleventh-century *Confessio*, or *Bosco Says* . . . the High King of Ireland, **Concubhar 'Frog Bags' Laoghaire**, made it official policy during that century to move strategic sites all over the place to confuse invaders. Hence, the diligent student will find that Dun Laoghaire was originally in County Mayo, Cork City was in County Waterford, and moves to relocate Cavan to the Atlantic seaboard failed – but not after several decades of trying. Sadly, as we know, Laoghaire was the second last High King in Ireland before Diarmuid Mac Murrough invited Strongbow over to sort out out a dispute he was having over a woman. The tradition of place-moving was outlawed, but not killed off, and persisted on a local level into the first quarter of the twentieth century. Many nineteenth-century books about the exploits of Resident Magistrates and their quaint Irish neighbours feature plots revolving around this practice – 12,738 of them to be exact, all of them dramatised by RTÉ at one time or another.

The problem with the centre of Ireland is not down to

official policy, but has more to do with lack of knowledge. Stupidity, if you will. Currently, this island's fulcrum is said to be located in County Offaly. Prior to this, Tara in County Meath was deemed to be at her centre, and for many years Athlone was jokingly referred to as the 'dead' centre of Ireland (until it twinned with Las Vegas in 1983 and became hip).

Many now believe that Emmet Square in Birr, County Offaly is built right smack in Mother Ireland's bellybutton and that this has always been the correct geographical location of her middle, except for a period of about 130 years. That particular span of time came about as a result of the overwhelming devotion shown by one of Daniel O'Connell's disciples.

Thomas Steele was an extraordinary individual – variously a Protestant landlord, duellist, underwater diving bell inventor, officer in the Spanish Constitutional Army and close friend of the man who won Catholic Emancipation for Ireland. Above all Steele was a passionate patriot and determined to do his best by his fellow man – except for the duelling bit. Ironically for a man who was an avowed pacifist he wasn't averse to firing off a pistol at dawn or financing military expeditions to Spain. It was the romantic, quixotic side to his nature that earned him the nicknames 'Mad' Tom or 'Honest' Tom Steele before he became the grandly-titled 'Head Pacificator of Ireland' during the Tithe Wars and the Repeal Years. Thousands of pages could – and should – be filled about this incredible character, who died lonely and miserable (but as time is ticking by and the author's tea is getting cold . . .).

Steele was a man who loved deeply. A good example of this was the mad, unrequited emotion he felt for a Miss Eileen Crowe of Ennis, County Clare. For hours on end, the lovesick landlord would stand on a rock in the River Fergus hoping to catch a glimpse of his beloved. When O'Connell told his friend that the woman wanted nothing to do with him, the pair fell out and didn't speak for a considerable time. It was only Steele's love for his leader that brought him around and the pair eventually made up, with the former forbidding any future mention of the subject. It was this fraternal affection that moved Steele to relocate the centre of Ireland to County Clare in honour of O'Connell. Sometime in the 1840s Steele removed a large stone from Birr, Co Offaly, which was known locally as the Seffin Stone. It was also called the '*Umbilicus Hiberniae*' or 'Navel of Ireland' and was said to mark the centre of the island. He had it transported to his estate at Cullane House by eight horses and set up as an altar upon which Mass was celebrated whenever O'Connell paid a visit. The stone was eventually returned to Birr in 1974 and most 'Biffos' still believe it marks the nation's centre point – which it doesn't.

According to the *CIA World Handbook*, Ireland is located at 53N and 8W. This is based on the approximate centre of the country as determined by the Agency's Nerd Unit. The coordinates of Birr, 53 06 10 N, put it about 9.6 km northeast of the CIA's marker. As only an idiot would argue with the CIA (remember the movie *Salvador* (1986)) this means that the Navel of Ireland should have been placed over the border in County Tipperary near an area known as Kilcunnahin Beg, not a million miles from the bustling hub of **Cloughjordan** and 0.65 km ESE of The Pike. Its elevation, to be thorough about this, is 150 m.

What's even more interesting about these figures is the fact that, from them, we can calculate the precise location of the **Anti-Ireland**. If you were to build a very large slingshot and fire yourself across the Atlantic and the USA, you would land (providing you had done your maths properly) in 53N, 172E – Ireland's opposite side of the Northern Hemisphere. Here you would need to hitch a lift in a fishing boat (as by now you would be drowning) and head 190 km east to the nearest dry land. You would then find yourself surrounded by seals and men in furry anoraks shivering a lot, as 53N and 172E is in the **Aleutian Islands** in the Bering Sea between Russia and Alaska. However, as the inhabitants spend all their time indoors, moaning about the weather, the Aleutians can hardly be considered to be the exact opposite of Ireland.

So where is the real Anti-Ireland? It can be found using the following experiment: take one moderately small beach ball, cover it with papier maché to represent islands, continents etc and plunge a knitting needle through the centre of Ireland at an angle representing 8.10 am/pm on the clock. The trick to avoid bursting the ball is to heat the needle first. Flipping the ball over you will see the tip pointing out at an island southwest of New Zealand at 53S and 172W.

As the Kiwis are really good at rugby, don't get sunburnt and were never conquered by the English, we can safely say that they are the true Anti-Irish and that New Zealand is the true Anti-Ireland – except for the unhealthy interest in sheep, of course.

INTERESTING FACTS

- Moving the centre of Ireland may have seemed pretty clever to a man who once made a poor busker 'Chief Musician of Ireland', but Tom Steele was only an amateur Place-Placer when compared to the Ordnance Survey of Ireland. In May 2006 the government agency managed to succeed where centuries of warfare had failed – and solved the Northern Ireland problem. Showing a mastery of illusion worthy of an Indian Fakir doing a rope trick, the OSI caused a commotion when they made the North disappear completely.

  As part of ongoing work on their new website, the surveyors published a series of 150-year-old maps minus the Six Counties. The maps were drawn between 1842 and 1913 – years before partition – which meant that they would originally have covered all 32 counties. The politically incorrect website, unsurprisingly, raised the hackles of Sinn Féin, with one member declaring the OSI actively supported partition. The row was defused when it was pointed out that that most of the North's maps had been taken off the OSI after partition was agreed – probably due to Unionist paranoia about Sinn Féin's forebears in the IRA. Still, for a while, it seemed like a really good idea.

• The OSI places the geographical centre of Ireland at 08W and 53 30N in the townland of Carnagh East, County Roscommon. This is on the western shore of Lough Ree, opposite the Cribby Islands and 8.8 km NNW of Athlone town. Again, we're sticking with the CIA.

Most Northerly Vineyard

Ireland is better known for the consumption of wine rather than its production. While wine sales slowed down in 2006 for the first time in a decade of massive growth, they still made up 16% of total alcohol sales, which is twice what it was in 1996. In one year alone, between 2003 and 2004, our glugging of fermented grape juice skyrocketed by 14.3%. Enough of the figures – we like our wine.

Our production of the same is so miniscule that most people don't realise that wet and windy Mother Ireland actually has over half a dozen small vineyards suckling at her earthy breast. If you find it hard to believe that Northern Europe could sustain grape growing, then a glance across the water at Britain will show you that wine production is on the increase in this part of the world. In 1988 there were 378 active British vineyards accounting for 382 hectares of vines in production. Seven years later the area in production had increased to 745 hectares, and the number of vineyards had increased to 419 and continues to rise. This is largely due to climate change and rising temperatures in the Northern Hemisphere.

Despite our relatively small landmass, with higher than average rainfalls and wind exposure, you may be even more surprised to learn that the European Commission has now officially listed Ireland as a wine–producing country. This is not a new thing however, as any amount of hopeful souls have attempted to grow grapes here over the centuries. Irish winemakers, for the record, tend to produce whites, which flies in the face of market trends because as a nation of bibbers we actually prefer reds.

The majority of vineyards are located in lush (pun intended) Munster. One of the earliest modern wineries can be found in one of the coach houses of Bunratty Castle in County Limerick. The Castle, which is famous for its 'begorrah banquets' aimed at American tourists, is also renowned for **Bunratty Mead**. Mead is a sweet honey wine and during the Middle Ages it was highly prized as a 'celebration drink', served almost exclusively at weddings, with a couple of bottles held over as a present for the newlyweds. Some claim this is where the word honeymoon comes from, the notion being that the flavoursome beverage would sustain the merry couple through a cycle of the moon. Others say it's from the tendency of the ancient Irish to drop their trousers and moon at passersby after a few bottles. Whatever the explanation, it's highly appropriate that one of Ireland's cheesiest venues should produce wine.

West Waterford Vineyard, near **Cappoquin**, draws on the mucky goodness of the fertile Blackwater Valley to make its wines and has an impressive 2,000 vines. The other, better-known vineyards are based in (the appropriately named) county of Cork.

Blackwater Valley Vineyard in **Mallow** has 2 hectares of vines and sells most of its bottles through the local shops. Smaller still is the vineyard in Longueville House, also in Mallow. Their 0.4 hectares of vines produce German Muller Thurgau and Reichensteiner grapes, Madeline Angevine from France and Early Calabrese from Italy which are winified and offered to diners in the estate's restaurant.

Further on out the road in Summercove in **Kinsale** the thirsty rambler can enjoy the fruity delights of a glass of Thomas Walk Vineyard's Amurensis tipple. Amurensis is named after the Amur Valley in northern China and is a species that remains inscrutable in the face of cold weather.

How it would stand up to the even cooler climes of Dublin's northside has yet to be tested. However, it would seem Madeleine Angevine and Pinot Noir like the vibe across the Liffey. The Fingal area is no stranger to winemaking and back in the eighteenth century there was a flourishing trade in booze production. And it's here that you will find Ireland's Most Northerly Vineyard –

in **Swords**. Horticulturist David Llewellyn's Fruit of the Vine winery takes a scientific approach to the art of wine-making. Apart from being planted with vines that are bred for cooler climes (Madeleine Angevine, Pinot Noir etc), Mr Llewellyn, who studied at UCD, has identified several 'hotspots' where vines will flourish on our dank island. He is, understandably, keeping the information to himself, but is quoted as saying that the areas where Ireland's current vineyards are located are not necessarily the best. Mr Llewellyn also makes a few bob from growing and selling vines, making apple juice and producing another Northside favourite – cider.

> The bad news is that the increase in the number of Irish vineyards is a sure sign that Global Warming has kicked in and the end of the world is at hand.

Despite our fondness for wine increasing with our relative wealth, we still love our beer – and more specifically our cider. In 2006 **Tipperary's Bulmers Cider** was still the fastest growing drinks brand in Ireland since the mid-1990s. Their Pint Bottle was also the biggest selling bottle of any beer on this island and, as a result of the brand's growth, the Irish are now the biggest per capita consumers of cider in the world.

So there you have it. We want the world to see us as sophisticated, wine-nosing Sommelliers, but in fact we're still a nation of bush drinkers. The bad news is that the increase in the number of Irish vineyards is a sure sign that Global Warming has kicked in and the end of the world is at hand. But don't worry, with all the extra wine on offer you won't feel a thing.

INTERESTING FACT

- Most of the world's grapes are grown between 30 and 50 degrees north or south of the equator. The world's most southerly vineyard is in the Central Otago region of New Zealand's South Island and the most northerly vineyard is Blaxsta Vingård in Flen, Sweden. And you thought Swede Wine was made out of turnips.

Rosiest
and Smelliest

Rosiest-Smelling Place

There are a number of prime candidates for this classification: the jacks in **Mother Kelly's pub** on Dublin's Talbot Street, due to the regular changing of the toilet cakes there or the **Rose of Tralee Festival**. Mind you, some of the contestants in the latter do smell a bit high, even before doing their jig/reciting their poem /playing their harp/disembowelling leprechauns/pole dancing etc on the stage in the Mount Brandon Hotel. Most of their 'rosy scent' is offset by the heady aroma of the Brut and Hai Karate aftershave worn by their testosterone-squirting 'escorts' as they try to impress their dates by out-head-banging each other to the Garda Band.

Another candidate must the **The Rose Garden** in **Raheny**, County Dublin. Dating from 1974, St Anne's is the biggest rose garden in the Republic of Ireland sprawling across 4 hectares. Its perfumed blooms do a creditable job of disguising the smell of cider during the long, hot summer months. However, it is not the Rosiest Smelling Place in Ireland. Neither are the capital's **Botanic Gardens** (founded in 1795 and handed over to the State in 1878). This flower arranger's paradise suffers from too much diversity and its 20 hectares on the Tolka flood plain are home to 20,000 living plants and half a million dried specimens in its herbarium (no Ganja, that we know of). As a rose specialist, it falls short of the mark.

There are three other gardens classified as 'botanic' in Ireland – they are the Talbot Gardens in Malahide, County Dublin, Trinity College Dublin Botanic Gardens and the Botanic Gardens in Belfast (5.5 hectares). It's to the latter city that we look for our nasal-flaring record of Rosiest-Smelling Place in Ireland.

More than 70,000 people visited the **City of Belfast International Rose Week** in July 2006 at Sir Thomas and Lady Dixon Park and if they didn't smell of roses when they arrived they stank of them when they left. With typical Northern fanatacism the organisers had lined up a staggering 45,000 different types of rose to sniff and coo over. There were red ones, white ones, pink ones, different shades of red ones, even more different shades of pink ones, not to mention the toffee-coloured ones. There were roses with pansy names like Buff Beauty, Ballerina and Honeybun, and roses with druggy-sounding labels like Purple Skyliners and Purple Tigers. There was even a rose without thorns (Tea Clipper's the name). Less pricks with the roses in Belfast?

Take note, Tralee.

INTERESTING FACTS

- The first pantomime staged in Ireland was performed at the Theatre Royal in Dublin in 1811. It was called *The Magic Rose*. Oh yes it was.

- In 1845 orchid seeds were germinated for the first time in cultivation at Dublin's Botanic Gardens. Potato blight was noted on 20 August of the same year . . .

Smelliest-Smelling Place

Like the entry for Rosiest-Smelling Place this category, too, has many ripe candidates. These include Dublin's now disused **Blackrock Baths** (on a sunny day when the tide is low), **Thurles**, County Tipperary, outside Moghler's former pub (as the abattoir lorry passes by), the **Culchie Festival** (wherever they hold it down the country) and **Mullingar** (for no particular reason).

The capital has many beauties to offer up. The quays have had their fair share of pongers, most notably back in the 1980s when the eggy whang off the Liffey, mixed with the oily bull-farts of the 7A bus on Eden Quay, would have choked a skunk. Then there was **Coolock** – the cheesiest and onioniest place in the country before they relocated the Tayto factory. More recently Ringsend has suffered from foul odours – some from the new sewage treatment plant, some from resident movie star Colin Farrell's aftershave.

Few people from the above parishes – or anywhere else in the country – would admit to living in a smelly dump, but this is not the case with the people of **Ballydonagh in Athlone**. Locals in the County Westmeath estate absolutely insist they are living in – or at least near to – **The Smelliest Dump in Ireland**.

According to a report in the *Irish Independent* in March 2005, home-owners there were kicking up a stink over An Bórd Pleanála's decision to grant permission to extend a 16-year-old tiphead off the Galway-Dublin Road.

The residents – most of whom were wearing clothes pegs on their noses – told the County Council that smells and gases coming from the dump 'would only turn your stomach', were noxious and would only worsen if the rank site was extended. People couldn't sleep at night or open their windows, and the kids were going up the walls.

Some of the councillors agreed that something had to be done about stinking Ballydonogh and one councillor, the spectacularly named Kevin 'Boxer' Moran, even offered to picket the site with the residents. Another councillor called for an environmental impact study to be undertaken in the area. One even went on record as saying the smell was so appalling that he couldn't

> More recently Ringsend has suffered from foul odours – some from the new sewage treatment plant, some from resident movie star Colin Farrell's aftershave.

understand how people lived there.

Following in the true community-minded spirit that makes all county councils countrywide so beloved of the voters, Westmeath's planners ignored everybody and went ahead and sought permission to extend the dump. The board duly allowed for the building of three new landfill cells, each about a half a hectare in size. While the landfill was expertly managed, everybody agreed that there was an appalling pong hanging over Ballydonogh (the council even spent over €500,000 trying to deal with it). On the basis that no one else would call their neighbourhood The Smelliest in Ireland, Athlone wins that title by a nose.

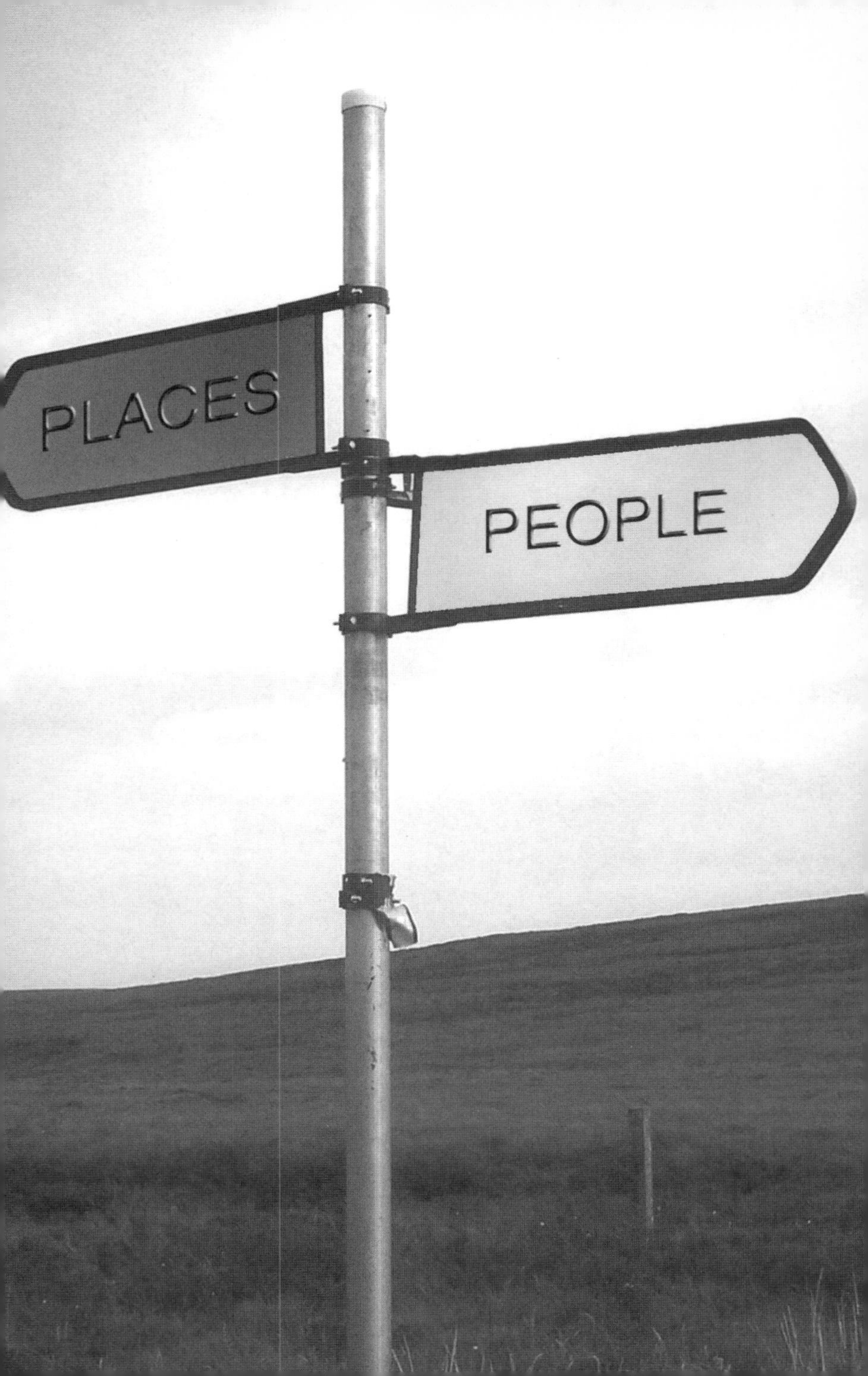
PLACES
PEOPLE

Best and Worst

Best Bertieism

Whatever you say about our intrepid leader, Patrick Bartholomew Ahern (born 1951), you have to admit he has a way with words – the wrong way. For the past 30 years since his election to the 21st Dáil on 16 June 1977, Bertie has astounded and delighted Leinster House with his mangling of the English language.

The 1977 election was the first time that 18-year-olds had their say at the polls, so perhaps his deft handling of monosyllables played well with the 'difficult' teen vote (one fifth of the electorate back then).

The following are some examples of Bertie's eloquent speechifying:

Appealing to Fine Gael TD Jim Mitchell in 1994: '*I* don't think it helps people to start throwing white elephants and red herrings at each other'.

On inflation, 14 July 2006: 'The reason it's on the rise is because probably the boom times are getting even more boomer.'

On his investigations into Ray Burke's murky past: 'I've looked up every tree in North Dublin.'

On politics, December 2000: 'Everyone knows the composition of the next Government will be decided by the electorate.'

On Dublin: 'Haughey wanted to transform Temple Bar into Ireland's West Bank.' (He succeeded.)

Then there was the interview he gave to *Hot Press* magazine in 1986 where he admitted that – at the age of 34 – he had never met a gay person, and looked up to Libyan dictator Colonel Muammar Gadaffi as a revolutionary hero (he'd stayed in his tent with him). More alarming was the admission that he could drive home after 'a fair few pints of Bass'.

As for spelling, there was the embarrassing incident regarding the phonetic rendering of the words 'Government' (spelt 'Goverment') and 'sympathy' (spelt 'sympaty') when written into the book of condolences for George Best in December 2005.

However, all the above oratorical and literary gems were mere beads and baubles when compared to the 24-carat diamond he dazzled the Dáil with during Leaders' Questions on 22 February 2006. In response to queries about the planning tribunal, Bertie defiantly told the House: 'I never condemn wrongdoing in any area.' [*Laughter*] 'Condone. I never condone wrongdoing.'

INTERESTING FACTS

- The 1977 FF election song, 'Your Kind of Country', performed by CT Wilkinson, was banned by CIE's piped-music department. Mr 'See Through Wilson', as he became known, went on to come fifth for Ireland in the 1978 Eurovision Song Contest with the song 'Born to Sing'. 'A man was born to do one thing and I was born to sing . . .' – evidently not on the buses though.

- The full exchange between Bertie and his fellow Deputies is textbook Dáil-speak, in so far as it makes absolutely no sense whatsoever, either in or out of context. Judge for yourself:

Mr. Sargent:	I am asking the Taoiseach what does he condone. That is my job here, to—
Mr. Gormley:	Hear, hear.
An Ceann Comhairle:	It is not a practice of the House to—
The Taoiseach:	I never condemn wrongdoing in any area.
Mr. Sargent:	The Taoiseach never condemns wrongdoing.
Mr. J. O'Keeffe:	The Taoiseach will meet himself coming back.

The Taoiseach: Condone. I never condone
                  wrongdoing. We set up the
                  Moriarty tribunal to inquire—

Mr. Boyle: The House set up the tribunal.

The Taoiseach: We set up the Mahon tribunal to
                  inquire into irregularities in the
                  planning—

Mr. Sargent: I am asking about the Taoiseach's
                  inquiry.

The Taoiseach: I will fill Deputy Sargent in on
                  my inquiry when he fills me in
                  on his inquiry—

[Interruptions – sound of toys being thrown out of prams]

Mr. Sargent: That is fair enough. The
                  Taoiseach can tell me about it.

Mr. Boyle: What does the Taoiseach need to
                  know?

Mr. Sargent: I would like to take the Taoiseach
                  up on his offer to tell me about
                  his inquiry.

[Inquiry? What inquiry?]

Mr. O'Donoghue: The fox in the hen house [?].

[More gobbledygook]

Mr. Sargent: I do not want things to fall
                  between stools. I want to make
                  sure that Fianna—

The Taoiseach: I am certainly sorry if one of my
                  party members caught Deputy
                  Sargent in —

Mr. O'Dea:　　　It was Giant Haystacks.

Mr. Eamon Ryan:　The Taoiseach was too busy signing blank cheques at the time.

Mr. J. O'Keeffe: This is a serious issue. . . This is not funny.

Best Untrue Bono Story

It is May 29 2005 and Bono, Economist Jeff Sachs, Bob Geldof and music producer Quincy Jones are in an audience with the Pope (who is wearing ox-blood coloured loafers). 'Those are some funky slippers,' Jones comments to Bono who is prancing about in his underpants.

Suddenly, JPII lunges at the U2 frontman and grabs his Blue-Fly shades, puts them on and grins mischievously.

'Hey Il Papa, no fair,' slurs Bono. 'Give me back my shades, dude!! And where are my trousers?'

The Pope shakes his head ruefully. 'Bleedin' rock stars,' he says. 'D'you not remember saying you wanted to swap them for me Rosemary Beads last night? You were gargled off your head, you mad thing.'

On hearing this Edge stops stroking his head with a toothless comb and Larry wipes some kebab sauce off his T Shirt. Could Bono really have given away his iconic shades, just like that?? What about the Rock and Roll Hall of Fame in Cleveland where they were destined to go on display for eternity? And did the Pope nick those natty shoes as well? The looked like a pair Adam used to wear in the Dandelion Market days?

'We'll see you in court!' the lads declare, before striking a post-modern ironic pose and leaving by the side door.

'See you in hell!!' roars the Pope, calling for his Swiss Guard. . . .

Too far-fetched, you say? Bono in his underpants? Edge using a comb on his shaved pate? Larry in need of a bib??

Now read on . . .

Best Headgear For Gig-Goers

Bono is responsible for many things: the previous section of text, the eradication of Third World debt, many fine musical moments, the death of the mullet (through overexposure) and the re-introduction of the cowboy hat as favourite headgear for concert-goers.

The cowboy hat was first made popular by Country and Western singer **TR Dallas** when he supported the Village People on their 1980 World Tour of the Midlands. TR was riding high in the charts at the time with his song 'Who Shot JR?', which cashed in on the plot line of a well-know American SOAP set in the oilfields of Texas.

Tom Allen (for that was his real name) hailed from the musical metropolis that is Moate and made his name on the Castleblayney circuit before being catapulted into the entertainment stratosphere during the Dallas madness that swept the country after an episode in which JR Ewing was shot. In June of 1980 he launched his new single and

---

[10] Swiss Guard is also the name of Dublin's bestselling haemorrhoid ointment. 'Soothes and Protects Your Swiss Roll' as the marketing slogan goes.

his new look (Danny de Vito with a Westmeath accent and cowboy hat) on *The Late Late Show* scoring a Top-100 hit in Britain. He followed this up with scores of others including: 'It's Hard to be Humble', 'Everyone's making it Big but Me', 'Daddy's Girl', 'Kisses on the Door' (?), 'Whiskey Castles', 'Big Tom Doesn't Play Here Anymore' and the raunchily titled 'The Last One to Touch Me'.

TR is now an auctioneer and Westmeath County Councillor, but his legacy is considerable. By the time he began touring with the Village People in 1980, the band's biggest hits were behind them and, sartorially, they had begun to slide too. Indian Guy had turned his back on his Native American heritage and was turning up for gigs in a blazer and grey flannels, Cop Guy had begun to look like a countrified member of An Garda Síochána, and Cowboy Guy had swapped his ten-gallon hat for a baseball cap with the 'Nilverm' logo emblazoned on it.

It was on the latter that TR's influence rubbed off most. After witnessing the power of the Moateman's Stetson over the countryfolk of Ballybofey etc, Cowboy Guy got back in the sartorial saddle and, with his Michael Guiney's hat perched jauntily atop his head, blazed the trail for urban cowboys everywhere.

The cool kids of rural Ireland weren't far behind in catching up on this latest fashion trend – besides, a good cowboy hat, unlike a cattle-drench baseball cap, is better for keeping the back of the neck dry as one snags turnips on a 'soft day'.

Throughout the summer of 1980, the young folk would sport nothing else on their curly-haired bonces when going to the local ballroom or GAA hop. Then, when the new series of Dallas was aired and viewers discovered that it wasn't TR Dallas who had shot 'ol' JR down, the craze died as quickly as you could holler 'yeeeeeeeeharrrr!!!!'. (The cowboy talk will cease from here on.)

Now, a quarter of a century on, a new generation of concert goer has rediscovered the cowboy hat and the joys of Post-Modern Irony. Now one can buy pink stetsons, red glittery stetsons, blue stetsons with spots, green stetsons with flashing lights, and gold straw Stetsons outside every major venue in Ireland, along with the last of the Choc Ices/Cheeky Charlies and strips of Sticking Plasters. And it's all thanks to Bono.

In July 2005 Bono battled it out in court with former U2 stylist **Lola Cashman** for the return of his pants, a sweatshirt and – most importantly – his stetson. In what ranks as one of the most bizarre cases in Irish legal history, the Dublin Circuit Court heard Ms Cashman deny that she had 'stolen' the wardrobe items following the band's Joshua Tree world tour in the mid-80s. The court also heard that the clothes, along with a pair of cheap costume earrings, had been offered for sale by Ms Cashman at a Christies rock memorabilia auction in 2002.

Lola – who had been employed to help create a new image for the band – claimed that Bono had 'gifted' her the items at the end of the tour. In particular she claimed the frontman had given her his hat on the last night in Arizona as he pranced about in his underpants.

For his part Bono told the court he had definitely never given her a present of his beloved hat and trousers, but might have told her she could have the earrings and sweatshirt, although he felt this was unlikely. The Fab Four told the court they would never have given the gear away as they would have wanted to keep them for their archives or for donations to rock and roll museums like the Hall of Fame in Cleveland.

Bono even compared the notion of giving away his famous stetson to that of the Edge giving away one of his guitars.

> **Bono even compared the notion of giving away his famous stetson to that of the Edge giving away one of his guitars.**

It had all started out so well. Bono had personally hired Lola in 1987 to replace their stylist who was on maternity leave and the famous Joshua Tree look (think straight *Brokeback Mountain* with anaemia) was born. In 1988 she parted company with the boys but had gathered enough 'material' to write a book *Inside the Zoo with U2*, in 2003. This tome allegedly detailed Bono's 'weight problems' among other fascinating items like Edge's comb missing some of its teeth and Larry's foodstained white T-shirts. It didn't, however, mention the night that knicker-clad Bono had allegedly given her his hat. When asked in court why the latter was the case, Ms Cashman replied that she wasn't writing a book about the gifts Bono gave her, adding, 'Your Honour, Bono would often prance around with his underpants on. If he had his underpants on, that was something for rock stars.'

While it may not surprise some to learn that rock stars
– like the rest of us – wear underpants (most of the time)
it might come as a bit of a revelation to learn that some
of Ms Cashman's subsequent clients had a penchant for
stetsons too. Two of these acts were **George Michael**
and **The Pet Shop Boys**.

George definitely has a bit of the cowboy in him (when
he's lucky) and The Pet Shop Boys' two biggest hits had
a western flavour – their version of the Willie Nelson
classic 'You Were Always on My Mind' and a low-camp
version of 'Go West'. The latter was, of course, one of
those hits that the Village People (the Casablanca LP,
1979) played during their tour of the midlands with TR
Dallas in 1980.

TR, for his part, still has his trusty old stetson, as does
the Cowboy Guy (along with his 'rusty sheriff's badge')
and Bono proved he loved his hat so much he was willing
to go to court for it.

With so many influential devotees, is it any wonder that
this style of hat is the Number One headgear for
concert-going mulchies wishing to emulate their heroes?

'Go West(meath), young man,' and all that.

Best Rebel Haircuts

Let's get this straight from the start – this entry is nothing
to do with **Sinéad O'Connor**. Yes, she is a bit of a rebel

and yes, she does have a famous hairstyle – or rather, lack of it – and yes, she has done more for slapheads than anybody else. It's just too obvious and, frankly boring, to say that Shinners has the most rebellious cut in Irish history (Pope picture-tearing incident notwithstanding).

The Best Rebel Haircuts in Irish history were those of the United Irishmen leadership in 1798. **Wolfe Tone, Lord Edward FitzGerald** *et al* sported a truly radical hairdo that rattled the English Establishment so much that anyone adopting it was liable to be arrested and tortured.

The 'do' in question was the kind of tightly-cut hairstyle that most conservative, 'respectable' people wear today. In the 1790s, when polite society all wore wigs and long hair, the 'new' style was associated with the anti-wig, anti-aristocrat luminaries of the French revolution. Having close-cropped hair implied sympathy with the pro-French United Irishmen and made the wearer fair game for a 'chat' with the Loyalist militia. During these interrogations suspects were routinely flogged, half-hung and 'pitch-capped'.

Pitch-capping was a singular innovation the British introduced to Ireland in the eighteenth century to deal with the uppity natives. The procedure first involved the shearing of the suspect's hair, which led to many ears being cut off. Then hot pitch (tar) was poured into a paper 'cap' and placed on the victim's head. After it had cooled and set, the pitch-cap was ripped off, taking the skin with it. Sometimes gunpowder was added to the pitch and the cap was set alight.

In some cases the victim's feet were untied so that the soldiers could have a bit of a laugh watching him running about in torment. In mitigation, this was in the days before TV.

The most famous pitch-capped United Irishman was the leader of the Boys of Wexford, **Anthony Perry**. The 'Screeching General', as he was nicknamed for his practice of shouting at the enemy, was born into the landed classes and went over to the rebels after witnessing the cruelty of the militia during the lead-up to 1798. He was arrested during the government's counter-insurgency campaign, tortured for 48 hours and pitch-capped. Understandably Perry broke and gave away some names. He was later released, but instead of going home to lick his wounds (which, being on his head, would have been difficult to do) he travelled to the rebel camp at Vinegar Hill and was appointed second-in-command to the North Wexford army. After a brave and Pyrrhically successful campaign he was captured and hanged. Poor Perry's hairstyle had, arguably, made him the **First Real Anti-Establishment Punk In Irish history**.

The close-cropped hairdos of Perry and the United Irishmen gave rise to the derogatory nickname 'croppy', which crops up in many old songs of the period: 'The Croppy Boy' and 'Croppies Lie Down' to name but two. The Croppy Acre is the name given to the site near Collins Barracks where the bodies of executed rebels were thrown into an unmarked pit during the rebellion.

Other Famous Rebellious Haircuts include the 'hairy

beardy bush' look beloved of **Mr Gerry Adams** and **Che Guevara**. Ernesto Guevara de la Serna was born in Argentina in 1928 of mixed Spanish and Irish Ancestry and could trace his roots to the Lynches of Galway. Prior to a chance meeting with Mr Adams in a County Clare pub in February 1960 he had favoured the croppy style but was so impressed with the Sinn Féin President's *gruaig* that he changed his look. He also adopted the nickname 'Che' after watching Cha and Miah in the original pilot of *Hall's Pictorial Weekly*.

Least Rebellious Haircuts

South Kerry's maverick political giant, **Jackie Healy-Rae**, has a hairdo that is really more of a hairdon't. His crowning glory looks like the early stages of pitch-capping and is an intriguingly constructed slick black swirl of something-that-resembles-hair. As he is an independent TD and has fought the government over various issues (such as the Smoking Ban) his 'do' qualifies as a Rebellious Haircut.

This is in stark contrast to fellow politico, Donie Cassidy. The senator, and showband supremo, is the bearer of Ireland's Least Rebellious Hairstyle. This is because his hairstyle is so perfect it looks like a wig. Wigs were, after all, what the croppies got all rebellious about in the first place.

INTERESTING FACTS

- At the time of writing, Jackie Healy-Rae is the oldest member of the Dáil at 75 years of age.
- Frank's satirical news programme *Hall's Pictorial Weekly*, which ran for 250 episodes until 1982, is widely credited with helping to collapse the 1973-77 Fine Gael-Labour Party coalition government. Its send-ups of Liam Cosgrave as Minister for Hardship, and Finance Minister Richie Ryan as Richie Ruin hit their marks so well that the coalition became a laughing stock with the public. Prior to this, political lampoonery was foreign to Irish TV screens. For all his rapier wit Frank Hall is also famous for not seeing the funny side of The Beatles when he interviewed them in November 1963 at Dublin Airport. He later dismissed them as 'monkeys'.

Best Live-Saving Dream

Back in the days when Perfidious Albion held sway in Erin, a Redcoat could stick a pike up you for even thinking about thinking about talking about rebelling. Therefore the indigenous Warrior Poet caste of old Ireland had to dream up some ingenious way of spreading sedition under the watchful ears of the Crown Forces. Lo and behold, the **Aisling Geal** was born. This is a coded 'vision' poem – it literally means 'shining vision' – that laments the days when Ireland's heroes were big enough and ugly enough to defend her honour. It usually involves some chap wandering about the place, taking a kip under a tree and being visited by a lovely shining woman (representing Mother Ireland) moaning at him to get up off his backside to rout the Ould Enemy. As most of the English back then didn't speak Irish, the Warrior Poets could probably have got away with saying anything they liked, but they were a wary bunch who didn't leave anything to chance. As a result, those Hessian swine who managed to translate an Aisling normally reported back to their superiors that the poems were all about some drunken paddy having a lewd dream about romping with a young one behind a bush. Or something like that.

The dream in an Aisling Geal may have led to the salvation of Erin, but the following young boy's dream lead to the salvation of his family. On 2 February 2006, the *Tallaght Echo* carried a story that must rate as the spookiest/most mysterious to grace the front page of an Irish newspaper in the first decade of this century. It concerned a family of eight from Killinarden that had a dramatic and singular escape from a house fire. According to the paper ten-year-old Rory[11] raised the alarm after waking up at 3.40 am to a smoke-filled house. However, it wasn't the smoke that had woken young Rory. It was a strange, troubling dream in which someone told him to get his family out of the house, that their lives were all in danger. The house was soon ablaze and dad, Martin, and

---

[11] The names of family members have been changed to respect their privacy,

mum, Deirdre, were trapped upstairs with their six kids. Brave dad managed to climb out onto the downstairs extension and land his three-year-old safely on some soft bags of rubbish in the garden. He then went back in to the house to save the others. By this time flames were coming into the bedroom and one of the girls was screaming after getting burnt on the hand. In true action hero style, Martin kicked the door shut and swung the kids on to the roof and dropped them down to the neighbours before jumping off with Deirdre.

If it hadn't been for Rory's weird dream . . . it doesn't bear thinking about, does it?

Stranger still is the fact that the 'B' family's fire brings to five the number of houses that have gone up in flames on the sixteen-house estate in the past number of years, leading residents to believe it is 'jinxed'. There were six fire-related deaths within a six and half year period, and two houses even went on fire twice. Could it have been a voice from the other side that stirred young Rory into action?

The family were treated in Tallaght Hospital for smoke inhalation after their ordeal. Despite this and the fact that their home was gutted, the 'Bs' counted their blessings. Everyone was alive and so 'all's well that ends well' etc.

Well, actually, no. That would be far too neat and tidy. Unbelievably, the 'Bs' returned from hospital to find that some skangers had stolen the children's bicycles from the front garden. One can only hope that the saddles were still hot.

INTERESTING FACTS

- Tallaght has the third largest population of any urban area in the Republic after Dublin and Cork City, but for some mad reason is still considered a town in the Greater Dublin Area. Back in the 1970s this sprawling conurbation at the foothills of the Wicklow and Dublin Mountains was only a small village, and now has a population of over 100,000 (Galway has 65,832 and Limerick has 54,023).

- Tallaght in Irish is Támhlacht, which means 'plague grave' and is mentioned in the *Book of Invasions* as being the burial place of thousands of the mythological Partholonians who were the second group to settle here after Noah's Flood.

- Tallaght gave its name to a Fine Gael strategy during the late 1980s which is credited with helping to give birth to the Celtic Tiger. The phrase 'Tallaght Speak' was coined in September 1987 when Alan Dukes delivered a speech to the Tallaght Chamber of Commerce. He outlined a policy whereby his party would not oppose economic reforms proposed by the Fianna Fáil government in the national interest. Prior to this, the indigenous 'Tallaght Speak' consisted of a few whistles and grunts and threats to break off various parts of your body. Or indeed, to 'burst' you.

Worst Irish King Of England Ever

Over the centuries Ireland has had a pretty bad run of luck with foreign kings – primarily those from England who didn't believe the natives were up to ruling themselves. However, on one occasion we did export a king of our own to Britain, although he didn't work out. The royal personage in question was **Lambert Simnel** (c.1475–1525) AKA Richard, Earl of York AKA Edward, Earl of Warwick, who was crowned King of England in Dublin in 1487. Lambert was so lousy at the job that he wound up as a kitchen porter, but more of that later.

This is how the story goes: Lambert Simnel was the happy-go-lucky son of an Oxford shoemaker who got caught up in the War of the Roses between the Houses of York and Lancaster. He was one of two so-called 'pretenders' to the throne of England who threatened the rule of that rather nasty piece of work, **Henry VII** (the other 'pretender' was a chap by the name of Perkin Warbeck). When he was ten Simnel was taken under the wing of a priest with the intriguing name of Roger Simon who set about turning his 'handsome' young charge into a king (could have been worse: he might have Rogered him into a queen). Planning to present Simnel as one of the sons of Edward IV, Simon, a particularly learned cleric, taught Simnel all the tricks of the court: how to bow, how to speak, how to dance etc. However, after hearing that **Edward, Earl of Warwick** (a genuine claimant to the throne) had been murdered in the Tower of London, Simon decided to introduce Simnel as the earl instead. At Simon's instigation rumours fled across the kingdom that Edward had survived the Tower and was now under the priest's protection (which he was not, as he was dead. Do try to keep up). Taking young Simnel across the Irish Sea the duo then sought out the Yorkist Earl of Kildare who decided he liked Simon's spin and agreed to support Lambert militarily, as did the young chap's 'aunt', Margaret of Anjou. She sent 2,000 German mercenaries under the generalship of one Martin Swartz to help him press his claim. The Jerries have always been helpful like that.

Now all they had to do was officially crown Simnel King of England, which they did to much ballyhoo on 24 May 1487 in Christchurch Cathedral. Hurrah! Hurrah! cried the people of Dublin. Afterwards they held a massive banquet in the Brazen Head with paper hats and Rice Krispie buns made out of potatoes.

Well, King Henry was neither gruntled nor commoded. He was, in fact, seething. Claiming that he still had the real Edward of Warwick in the Tower, he paraded the young boy around to show Simnel up as an imposter. Then the Earl of Lincoln (who had a claim on the throne himself) threw himself behind Simnel, fled to Flanders and from there travelled to Ireland to join the young king-in-waiting and the Earl of Kildare's forces. The blood was up, boys (as they said back then) – the Paddys were about to invade England.

Worst Irish Invasion Of England Ever

Yes, yes, we've all heard the words 'invasion' and 'Irish' used before in the same sentence, but it normally refers to soccer supporters travelling to away games, punters heading to Cheltenham or navvies looking for work in Birmingham. Few remember the fact that from antiquity through the Middle Ages Irish slave-trading invaders put the willies (not literally) up the English and the Welsh with their constant raiding.

The largest Irish-led army ever to invade Britain was 4,000-strong and led by the Lord Chancellor of Ireland, Sir Thomas Fitzgerald (and young Simnel of course). These were 'Kern' infantry, who were renowned and feared for their mobility and their prowess at close quarter fighting. Fitzgerald was joined by Swartz's 2,000 mercenaries and as many English retainers. They landed on 4 June 1487 near Barrow-in-Furness and travelled on to Masham in Yorkshire and, marching southwards, crossed the Trent near East Stoke. In the meantime, Henry VII had been gathering his forces and marched northwards to meet them with an estimated 12,000 men.

The Irish covered an impressive 320 km (200 miles back then) in only five days and had their first taste of action on 10 June when 2,000 of their number overwhelmed 400 Lancastrians on Bramham Moor. Thereafter they scored a number of victories against the king's forces including a successful three days skirmishing with the enemy in Sherwood Forest. However, the latter had slowed them down to such an extent that Henry was able to receive reinforcements and on 16 June the decisive battle was fought at Stoke Fields near the village of East Stoke.

At about 9 am the vanguard of the king's troops came upon the Irish massed on the brow of a hill which was protected on three sides by the river Trent. They had been celebrating Bloomsday and fighting over who was getting the last fried kidney when the English charged. Leaving the washing-up to one side, the rebels streamed downhill and relinquished their superior position on the higher ground. It was a disastrous move and the battle, which raged for three hours, saw 4,000 of the Irish force cut down – their lack of body armour had proved their undoing, despite their lauded skill and bravery. All the rebel leaders died fighting. 3,000 of Henry's men also bit the turf.

This was to be the last battle of the War of the Roses and Henry's crown was safe-ish.

Father Simon avoided the chop due to his status as a priest, but was jailed for life. The young Simnel was pardoned because of his age and was given a humiliating job in the king's kitchens, later becoming a royal falconer. He died 50 years after the battle of Stoke Fields in 1534 and became known throughout history as both the Worst Irish King of England and also **The Most Overqualified Pot-Walloper**.

But Lambert's wasn't the only failed attempt by an Irish army to invade crown territory. There was also the time we invaded Canada.

Worst Irish Invasion Of Canada Ever

On 1 June 1866 a force of highly-trained Civil War-hardened Fenians under **General John O'Neill** invaded Canada, capturing a fort in their first engagement and creating military history in their second.

The Fenian Movement, as you history buffs know, was a trans-Atlantic revolutionary organisation that drew its resources from the Irish–American immigrant community. They saw the start of the American Civil War in 1861 as an opportunity to train regiments of Irish volunteers who would fight for the Union and then return to liberate Ireland. However, the war lasted too long and the organisation was compromised, which led to a split (sounds familiar, doesn't it?) with one side deciding to rearm and invade southern Canada. Once there, an Irish Republic in Exile was to be proclaimed which would either draw troops away from Ireland or be used as leverage in negotiations with the British. Luckily for them, the US government was still annoyed with Britain for selling arms to the Confederacy and so would turn a blind eye to the expected invasion of one of her colonies.

The Fenian band set out from Buffalo and other points along the Niagara frontier, landing in Ontario where they took Fort Erie. From there they headed north with the aim of capturing the strategic Welland Canal that connects the lakes Erie and Ontario.

On their way they encountered a force of English colonials and made history by breaking the legendary

'British Square'. This was a highly-disciplined infantry formation of hollow squares that had withstood Napoleon's cavalry charges at the Battle of Waterloo and was, apparently, unbreakable. The English left the field to the Fenians who, disappointingly, didn't follow up on their success. With more crown soldiers on the way and the border sealed by President Andrew Johnston's government, the leadership decided to withdraw across the Niagara River and spent the next few years making incursions and further plans to invade. As a result, the Empire of Canada still persists to this day.

Eventually the Fenians went underground, becoming the Irish Republican Brotherhood (IRB) and 60 years after the Battle of Ridgeway they organised the Easter Rising, which was the **Best Ever Irish Invasion of O'Connell Street** (Outside Of When The Country Folk Come Up To Shop In Clery's On 8 December).

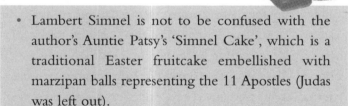

INTERESTING FACTS

- Lambert Simnel is not to be confused with the author's Auntie Patsy's 'Simnel Cake', which is a traditional Easter fruitcake embellished with marzipan balls representing the 11 Apostles (Judas was left out).

- On spotting a billboard with the legend 'Drink Canada Dry' while touring North America, Brendan Behan is reported to have quipped: 'Drink Canada Dry? Alright, I'll give it a go.'

Worst Thing To Do With A Corpse's Head

Play football with it. The mummies of St Michan's Church in Dublin laid undisturbed for hundreds of years, even despite shelling during the Civil War assault on the Four Courts – that is until a group of teenagers decided to alleviate their boredom by breaking into the crypt in July 1996.

The church dates from 1095 and stands on the site of a structure erected by Dublin's vikings who had been booted out of the walled city. The mummies in question include a 400-year-old nun, 2.5-metre crusader (who had to be bisected to fit him into his coffin) two executed leaders of the 1798 rebellion (the Sheare brothers) and a man, possibly a thief, with one hand and both of his feet chopped off. Their state of preservation is down to the limestone in the walls of the church, which keeps the air dry.

But enough of the science. All the wonders of nature couldn't protect them from the depredations of our cut-price trio of Indiana Joneses. The thrill-seekers broke into the crypt after reading an article in a red-top newspaper about possible treasures buried on the church grounds. After failing to find any, they decided to have a little 'fun' with the corpses and played footie with the head of a mummified baby. The little body was taken from a coffin marked 'E. Hall, died 1838, aged four months'.

Leaving a trail of destruction in their wake – some of the sixty destroyed coffins dated from 1680 – they also managed to start a fire, which caused even more damage.

The church managed to salvage some of the coffins and their remains, and reburied them before sealing the vault. After pleading guilty to arson, theft and criminal damages charges, one of the boys was sentenced to six years, which was later – like the crusader – cut in half.

Commentators afterwards agreed that 'he was one reckless mummies boy'.

Best Thing To Do With A Corpseless Head

Ship it off to Drogheda and bung it in a shrine. This is what happened to the noggin of **St Oliver Plunkett** after he shared the same fate as the Sheare brothers of St Michan's – being hanged, drawn and quartered by the English in 1681. Saint Oliver had the misfortune of being born during the time of the Penal Laws, when the Catholic Church and her ministers were suppressed. Despite this, the saintly Meathman (and there aren't too many of them) worked tirelessly in the pastoral care of his flock. At first he was able to work openly but later, when the political situation changed, he went into hiding. Even then, at great peril to himself, he continued to minister on.

When he was appointed Archbishop of Armagh in 1669, the price on his head rose from £5.00 (for lowly priests) to £10.00 (for bishops). Ten years later he was arrested on trumped-up charges relating to a 'Romish plot' and, after one of the most notorious mis-trials in British legal history, was sent to Tyburn to be hanged, drawn and quartered. Most onlookers believed that – mercifully – he didn't live long enough to see his innards being drawn out and lobbed into the fire. One **Elizabeth Shelton**, from a highly regarded Catholic family, succeeded in petitioning the king to recover the remains immediately after the execution. She was given Plunkett's head and other 'quarters' after the bowels had been cast into the flames. (Would she really have wanted to keep his bowels?) Saving these charming items in two tin boxes, she had them certified by a surgeon named John Ridley. The relics were eventually entrusted to the Siena Nuns (of the Dominican Convent at Drogheda, County Louth) and are presently enshrined in St Peter's Church, as is the door of the cell St Oliver occupied at Newgate prison.

> Looking a little like a giant raisin, brave Saint Ollie's bonce peers out of a huge gilded case and is a perennial favourite with children on school tours.

Looking a little like a giant raisin, brave Saint Ollie's bonce peers out of a huge gilded case and is a perennial favourite with children on school tours.

Legend has it that a bearded, and 'well-locked', member of a famous folk group once made an American tourist faint with fright when he hid behind the reliquary and moaned, 'OOOOOOOOH, me headddd . . .'

With this in mind, we should be thankful that Ms Shelton didn't manage to rescue St Oliver's bowels.

Worst Thing To Do With Your Head In The Vicinity Of A Headless Corpse

Get it stuck on a spike, as did little Sophie Flanagan of St Michan's House flat complex in Dublin in September 1996. She spent over an hour with her head impaled on a 30 cm metal spike, which pierced her bottom jaw and came out through the side of her cheek.

The plucky young Dub and her friend had been playing in the Greek Street area of the inner city and climbed over a locked gate to get home into St Michan's House. Unfortunately, Sophie slipped and fell down on the pointed spike.

Amazingly, the brave five-year-old never cried once, although she was conscious right throughout the ordeal as firemen worked to free her. Her rescuers couldn't remove the spike (which had knocked out her front teeth out and passed dangerously close to her windpipe) so they had to cut away the whole gate and bring her to hospital lying on the railings with the spike still in her jaw. Hospital staff praised Sophie as one of the most courageous little girls they had ever treated.

INTERESTING FACTS

- The St. Michan's organ is one of the oldest in the country still in use. It is believed that George F Handel played it when composing *The Messiah*.
- In times past it was said to be good luck to shake the leathery hands of the crusader in the crypt.
- 'Spike' is what American footballers do when they score a touchdown, i.e. they drive the ball into the ground.

Worst Irish Turkishman

This title is held by the magnificently-named **Dr Achmet Borumbad**, who arrived in Ireland as a refugee in the late eighteenth century. He was said to be a very large, bearded gentleman who was wont to wander about the city streets in his native robes.

The doctor became such a well-known figure that he managed to persuade some other members of the medical profession and the House of Commons to finance his plans for a Turkish bathhouse at Bachelor's Walk. This singular amenity used hot and cold seawater treatments and was connected to the Liffey, which at high tide refreshed the Doctor's 'cool pool'. Like Borumbad, the Bachelor's Walk Turkish Baths became an overnight sensation. However, he was constantly broke and wore a path to parliament looking for extra funding for his project. His friends never let him down, until an incident occurred that was to change his fortunes permanently.

It was Achmet's practice to throw lavish feasts at the baths to soften up his MP chums prior to a begging mission to College Green. On what proved to be the last such occasion, Borumbad was pouring wine into a group of thirty law makers when events took an almost fatal turn. The elderly and very drunk **Sir John Hamilton** decided to call it a night and leave before things got out of hand. Opening the wrong door on his way out he fell into the huge, cold salt-water bath. On hearing his screams, eighteen of the younger party-goers rushed to his aid and promptly fell in as well. If that wasn't enough to sour relations, it was then discovered that the only dry clothes on the premises were of the native Turkish variety. The dripping MPs were subsequently forced to head home, carried on sedan chairs dressed in the fetching, and very vibrant, robes.

Borumbad's benefactors subsequently refused to fund his business and he cast around for a new 'cash cow '. This he found in the ample charms of a Miss Hartigan, sister of a well-known surgeon. At first she found his Turkish charms delightful but refused to have anything to do with him unless he shaved off his beard and converted to Christianity. He duly obliged and, with some relief, threw off his Oriental garb to reveal himself to be the very un-Turkish Paddy Joyce from Kilkenny. 'Divil the Turk I am!' quoth he, before (presumably) leaping on Miss Hartigan and ravishing her. Paddy had apparently got the idea for the bathhouse when he was in Turkey on his holidays.

Best Northside Dalai Lama

Another Dublin doctor of note – **Tuesday Lobsang Rampa** of Howth – had rather more success in attracting money than the aforementioned Paddy Joyce. The Buddhist philosopher, who made a good living from writing on the occult, arrived in Dublin in the 1950s after an astral visit by the Dalai Lama who told him to go to the Green City with his wife and his telepathic Siamese Cat. Once in the capital he rented rooms near Trinity College and later moved Northside when writing his book *The Doctor from Lhasa*. He settled in well and there was nothing he liked more than to take a drive into the Dublin Mountains and enjoy the scenery. Sometimes he would even 'fly' there at night (apparently he could run through the air at 640 km an hour), and on one occasion he came across an abandoned Siamese cat which he named Mrs Fifi Greywhiskers.

Mrs Fifi (presumably she was divorced) used to act as a medium for the Dalai Llama to communicate with Lobsang. Co-incidentally after a hefty tax bill dropped on the philosopher's doormat in the mid 1970s, Mrs Fifi got a call from the Dalai Lama telling her owner (and recent author of *The Third Eye*) to hightail it to The Land of The Red Indians – Canada. Lobsang reluctantly did so by airplane (as unfortunately 'seagulls had bent the rods of my astral aerial', he explained). Lobsang continued to write over a dozen books until his death in 1981.

No one was surprised when Dr Tuesday Lobsang Rampa was revealed, during his life to be a plumber named Cyril Henry Hoskins who had shaved his head, bought some Buddhist robes and spent a lot of time in London's libraries. Laudably, the 'spiritualist', who had never been to Tibet, claimed that although on the outside he was from Devon he had become possessed by a Lama's spirit after falling out of a tree.

Best Irish Englishman For Being A Bad Italian

The case of our toothless Republic of Ireland soccer hero **Tony Cascarino** is the final proof that the Irish love a chancer. Like many other members of **Jack Charlton's** world-beating side of the 1980s and 1990s, the soccer star was as Irish as warm beer and jellied eels.

Anthony Guy Cascarino (born 1 September 1962 in St Paul's Cray, near Orpington, Kent, England) represented Ireland sixty-six times – qualifying through his Irish grandmother. He scored nineteen goals mainly through his aerial prowess, which was perfectly suited to Jack's 'put them under pressure' long ball game. Big Tony was an integral part of the team and deserves his place in Irish sporting lore. It was only after he retired that he remembered to tell everyone that his mother was adopted, which would have disqualified him from playing in the green shirt. On the other hand with a name like Cascarino he could have qualified for the Azurri.

Still Italy's loss was Ireland's gain. Go on you good thing, etc. and so forth.

INTERESTING FACT

• The first Turkish Delight chocolate was made in Cobh, County Cork, by the Hadji Bey company in the 1890s.

Worst Mayors Of Dublin

Many Dubliners would be of the opinion that Fianna Fáil Young Turk, **Royston Brady**, is the only candidate for this title, but the office of mayor has been held by several hundred top-class toss-pots since it was created almost 800 years ago.

The post of Mayor of Dublin was created in June 1229 by Prince Henry III, and first occupied by a gentleman by the name of Richard Muton. The position was elevated by royal decree to 'Lord' Mayor in 1665 when Sir Daniel Bellingham took office and the last 'ordinary' Mayor, William Smyth, stood down. Since then 377 men and women have worn the Lord Mayoral chain around their thick necks.

The Lord Mayor is the First Citizen of Dublin, ranking second only to the President of Ireland within the boundaries of the capital and is afforded equal status as the Taoiseach at official functions. He or she chairs all Dublin City Council Meetings and is elected by his or her fellow councillors in June each year. The job also comes with the added perk of a casting vote in the event of deadlock at council meetings, a fantastic *pied à terre* (the Mansion House on Dawson Street) and a nice little run-around (the gold coach/BMW car with personal driver).

The aforementioned Royston's political career kicked off in May 1999 when he quit his hotel management job and was elected a councillor for the North Inner City Ward at the first attempt. Within a year he was installed as Deputy Lord Mayor to Bertie Ahern's big brother, Maurice, as part of a Fianna Fáil/Labour agreement to share the Mansion House. In 2003 he got the main gig himself and was well on his way to political stardom. Some even whispered that he might be a future leader of The Republican Party because of his friendship with Bertie. Royston's older brother Cyprian (he also has a brother called Fulton and a sister named Perpetua) was one of Bertie's Praetorian Guard at his Drumcondra Clinic, St Luke's. At the age of eleven, Royston was doing leaflet drops for the future Taoiseach and endearing himself to Bertie's then girlfriend, Celia Larkin, when he should have been out making a nuisance of himself like other kids his age. It all went horribly wrong when he walked through the doors of the Mansion House.

Within a year of being made mayor, Royston had become The Most Ridiculed First Citizen in the history of the job. His propensity for political gaffes and love of publicity made him a constant target for criticism. During his 'reign' he was, among other things: made to apologise to Justice Minister **Michael McDowell** for

149

calling him an arrogant bully; ticked off for missing city council meetings; rapped for using the state coach (built in 1780) at his wedding; and accused of pulling a publicity stunt by allowing two homeless people marry in the Mansion House. He also annoyed ferret-faced Minister for Health, Micheál Martin, when he got behind the publicans as they were fighting with him over the smoking ban.

One angry former Lord Mayor, **Dermot Lacey** (Labour) even wrote to the *Sunday Independent* over an article which stated that Royston was 'the most successful Lord Mayor in recent years'. According to Cllr Lacey the role of mayor was devalued repeatedly during Brady's tenure and he accused him of being more interested in getting his face in *VIP* magazine than actually contributing anything to the future of Dublin. The rest of the letter was equally excoriating.

So sustained was the criticism of Royston that he even became a yardstick for measuring everything that was wrong with the system of electing mayors. At the Progressive Democrats Annual Conference in March 2004, one member, Tony Williams, told his audience that local government should be reformed and that direct elections were the only way to boot the Royston Bradys out of politics. Brady, he said, 'is what you get when you demean, diminish and strip of its powers the ancient office of Lord Mayor of Dublin, when you leave it as a cheap bauble, a gift, a plaything, something to be carved up by Fianna Fáil and Labour'.

Royston finally came unstuck when he decided to run

for the European Parliament at the end of his term. In the run-up to the elections he did an interview with the *Sunday Independent* in which he stated that his dad had been abducted by the Dublin–Monaghan bombers in 1974 and his taxi used as the getaway car. Unable to substantiate the getaway car part of the story, he flopped at the polls. So that was the end of Royston. Or was it?

In 2006 Brady made a comeback of sorts when he judged the Rose of Tralee contest. The potted biography on RTÉ's website described the former Rose escort as a 'qualified hotelier' and 'accomplished politician'. As ever, Royston was keeping his options open.

Whatever about his political achievements, Royston Brady added to the gaiety of the nation, not least for his acute political observations. In January 2004 he memorably described the 'pathetic' city councillors of Dublin as 'clowns' and 'a waste of space'. The uproar was hilarious. He was, of course, bang on the mark although the description might have easily applied to himself.

> The potted biography on RTÉ's website described the former Rose escort as a 'qualified hotelier' and 'accomplished politician'. As ever, Royston was keeping his options open.

While he definitely wasn't The Most Successful Lord Mayor Ever he was certainly The Worst Mayor For Getting Slagged Off. Which was something you wouldn't dare do to the extremely sensitive Alderman **Sir Michael Creagh** . . .

Worst Mayor For Over-Reacting

1688 was a bad year for the bell-ringers of Dublin. In fact it was a bad year for everyone in Dublin as it ushered in the reign of the obnoxiously sycophantic Sir Michael Creagh. A fanatical royalist, the incensed Creagh sent his soldiers around to Christ Church Cathedral to tell the ringers that the bells had not been rung 'merrily enough' to celebrate the birth of the Prince of Wales that year. (This might be where the expression to 'come out fighting at the bell' originated, or possibly not.) The officers of the cathedral, naturally, denied the charge adding that if this was the case then it was the ringers' fault, not theirs. Creagh, who may have been a bit fond of the sauce, had them dragged off to the stocks while the ringers gratefully tugged and yanked their ropes to express their appreciation. Creagh was a pussycat, however, compared to his predecessor **Walter Ball** . . .

Worst Mayor For Being An Utter Bastard

The truly foul Walter Ball was definitely not the kind of man you should invite around for tea, as his mother Margaret discovered to her detriment. In 1584 Ball callously martyred the unfortunate old lady in the cold, dark dungeons of Dublin Castle during the Tudor persecution of Roman Catholics.

In 1536 Parliament declared Henry VIII to be the supreme head of the Church of Ireland and that anyone who said otherwise or continued to obey the Pope could be put to death. When Henry's daughter **Elizabeth I** came to power she vigourously pursued this policy and added an extra 'rider': that anyone refusing to swear an oath to her as head of the church would not be allowed hold religious or political office. This would eventually lead to Margaret's imprisonment and death.

The Meathwoman had moved to Dublin in 1530 at the age of sixteen with her wealthy new husband, Bartholomew Ball, the man responsible for building the bridge over the Dodder that still bears his name – Ballsbridge. Bartholomew, a Catholic, was elected Mayor in 1553, five years before Elizabeth took the throne. Both he and his wife were staunch supporters of the Church of Rome and Margaret held Masses and cathecism classes in her home. Her husband's high status offered her the protection to practice her faith but when he died in the late 1560s she was left exposed and liable to the 'chop'. She had no idea then that the official responsible for her death would be her own son, Walter.

Walter Ball wanted to follow in daddy's footsteps and become Lord Mayor, so he renounced Catholicism and took the oath of supremacy despite the best efforts of his mother to dissuade him. For Walter, political ambition outweighed everything else, his mother and soul included. In 1577 he was appointed Commissioner for Ecclesiastical Causes and her fate/faith was sealed.

Margaret continued to invite him around to the family home to dine with whatever fugitive cleric she was sheltering at the time. Walter didn't reconvert however, but accepted the invitations to gather information about wanted clergymen.

In 1580 he was made Mayor of Dublin and celebrated by arriving at his mother's house with a company of soldiers. Margaret was celebrating Mass with her chaplain when Walter came calling earlier than expected. The treacherous First Citizen arrested them and flung his mother into the castle dungeons. As an extra humiliation he had her dragged through the streets on a makeshift cart as she was unable to walk.

Now ordinarily, when someone throws their 65-year-old mother in jail they might be expected to admit that they're a bit of a bastard – it being a bit extreme and all that. They might even joke that it's one less bus pass for the state to worry about. Not Walter. He reckoned he was doing Margaret a favour as she should have been executed for attending Mass. He had 'spared her'. When his siblings protested, he replied that she would be allowed to go free if she renounced Catholicism, which she refused to do.

Even when her other sympathetic son Nicholas was elected Mayor in 1582 Walter refused to budge. As he was still the royally-appointed Commissioner for Ecclesiastical Causes he outranked his brother and thwarted all his efforts to release her. She must take the oath to Elizabeth or die in the dungeons. Margaret opted for the latter and passed away in 1584 at the age of 69, crippled with arthritis. Extraordinarily, she had bequeathed her property to Walter.

As he was brutal with dealing with OAPs, Walter – not the colourful Royston Brady – is The Worst Mayor of Dublin Ever. During his term of office Brady never once threw his mother in jail for anything. Not even for christening him Royston.

INTERESTING FACTS

- On 20 June of the same year that Margaret Ball died, the Archbishop of Cashel, Dermot O'Hurley, was martyred at Hoggen Green on Dame Street. He had been horribly tortured using the 'boot'. This involved placing the prisoner's legs in two topboots, which were then filled with pitch, tar, bitumen and salt amongst other things. The boots were then placed over a fire until the victim's legs were roasted to the bone and stripped of tissue. Another Mayor of Dublin, Francis Taylor was condemned to the dungeons after exposing electoral fraud and refusing to take the oath. He died in Dublin Castle in 1621. In September 1992 the brave trio were beatified by the Church.

- Daniel O'Connell became the first Catholic Lord Mayor since 1690 when he was elected in 1841. The first female Lord Mayor was Kathleen Clarke (1939) and the first Jewish Mayor was Bob Briscoe (1961). The second was his son, Ben (1988).

- The 377th Lord Mayor of Dublin, Cllr Vincent Jackson had his name pulled from a hat after he tied on 26 votes with the front-runner candidate, Cllr Paddy Bourke of Labour.

Worst Baby-Faced Litter Bug

As if to prove that Royston Brady was absolutely correct in referring to council officials as 'clowns', the capital's bureaucrats donned their reds noses and unicycled into the headlines again in August 2006. According to the *Irish Sun* a family from East Wall were 'gobsmacked' when they received an official letter demanding payment of a fine for illegal dumping. They were, unsurprisingly, furious at the suggestion that one of their family members would be responsible for such a serious crime and claimed their rubbish had been tampered with. This may sound like a run-of-the-mill appeal over a fine and would have been just that except for one thing – the dirty litter bug in question was a baby.

Council staff had found a bag of rubbish that appeared to have been illegally dumped and discovered the name and address of the baby on paperwork inside the sack. They then despatched a fine by post, which arrived just before the little girl's first birthday making her The Youngest Person Ever To Be Fined For Littering. The man of the house claimed he telephoned the council expecting them to drop the matter immediately but was taken aback when told by an official that he would have to formally appeal against the fine. The matter would then be reviewed.

On hearing the council's response the mini-villain flew into a rage, threw her 'boo' on the floor and burbled, 'Ga-ga' – which sums up the whole affair nicely.

Another unlikely crime figure is the elusive Enya. The singer was behind a multi-billion dollar heist in

Singapore in 1999 where the perpetrators got away scot-free and ended up falling in love with each other. True story.

Well maybe not exactly 'true' per se. A CD of her music was used to crash the mainframe of a trading bank in the Far East in the awful caper flick *Entrapment*, starring Catherine Zeta Jones and Sean Connery. The council have no plans to investigate at time of writing.

INTERESTING FACT

- In 2006 the council spent up to 20 hours of each 24 hours collecting litter and spent €20m on street cleaning removing 20,000 tonnes of rubbish which included 130 million plastic bags.

Worst Impressions Of Ireland Ever

For an island its size (70,280 sq km – 1,390 sq km of which is under water), Ireland has always demanded a disproportionate amount of attention from the rest of the world. At least 3.2 gazillion books, plays and songs have been written about this tiny damp spot on Europe's outskirts. Iceland, Denmark and even Wales don't seem to command the same interest. So why do the Irish?

The answer to this lies in our troubled history. Having been raided and invaded more times than any other place anywhere in the world – ever – the Irish, over the centuries, have developed the skills necessary to win over their conquerors. The Vikings, the Normans and even the English all succumbed to our charms and in the case of the first two actually went native. This is down to the Irishman's ability to sing and dance, tell an ould yarn and be quaint – all at the drop of a flat cap. Over the centuries the Irish became the loveable rogues of the world, constantly entertaining the hordes of rapists and plunderers who landed on their shores. If Ireland were a person, she would be your precocious, curly-haired niece who is trundled out at family gatherings to sing show-tunes from *Annie, The Musical*: 'Da sun will come OOOUUUTT tomarraaaaaa AAAAAGGHHHHH'. You know how it goes.

Everybody loves the Irish; everybody hates the Americans; the English think everybody loves them; the Germans won't stop apologising for being German; and everybody looks down on the Welsh – but everybody loves the Irish. And the Irish love to be loved (except by each other). That's why when anyone says horrible things about us we take such great exception.

THE COLUMNIST – Take **Robert Kilroy-Silke**, English TV presenter and columnist/politician. In 1992 he made

> . . . everybody hates the Americans; the English think everybody loves them; the Germans won't stop apologising for being German; and everybody looks down on the Welsh – but everybody loves the Irish.

a comment about Ireland in his *Daily Express* column, which stated that EU Commissioner Ray MacSharry was a 'redundant second-rate politician from a country peopled by priests, peasants and pixies'.

There was such a huge outcry in Britain's Irish community and throughout the Auld Sod itself that Ireland's Ambassador to Britain, Joseph Small, condemned the 'gratuitously offensive, and indeed, racist, remarks'. The *Daily Express* was forced to apologise to Mr MacSharry and the Irish people in general. Everybody agreed that it had been an incredibly stupid thing to say as there are no pixies in Ireland, only Leprechauns.

Kilroy-Silke later went on to win over the Muslims by saying that Arabs should go down on their knees and thank God for the 'munificence' of the USA. Which God wasn't specified.

THE TV PROGRAMME – The BBC series *EastEnders* also created a furore when it set a few episodes in Ireland. Its portrayal of the Paddys was spectacularly off the mark for a show set in a country where the biggest ethnic grouping is Irish. The BBC was so embarrassed by the Oirishness of the scenes that it took the unprecedented step of airing the following introduction to the programme:

> Tonight's episode of *EastEnders* contains scenes that may offend some viewers. The BBC has apologised if they offended Irish people, as they have no wish to misrepresent them. The BBC would like to assure viewers that there was no intention to upset anyone through the portrayal of the Irish visit and they apologise to anyone who has been.

The plot involves the ever-miserable Pauline Fowler and her family travelling to Ireland in search of a long-lost daughter/pot of gold/acting teacher/whatever. Before old misery guts even sets a foot out of her minivan her family witnesses two men engaged in a public row. This 'Fighting Irish' vista is made even more hilarious because while the arguing is going on, the townspeople are busy trying to fob off their livestock in the village square. Would your honour like to buy a sheep? and so on. To add insult to injury, while the village idiots carry on behaving like characters out of a Somerville and Ross novel, English sophisticates Pauline and Ian Beale share a heart-to-heart about the meaning of life, the universe etc.

Then there's the stupid innkeeper, who is unable to understand that the Towlers are the Fowlers, and that someone has written their name down incorrectly on the reservation forms. Mark Fowler humours the old fool saying that his family will vacate the rooms when the 'Towlers' arrive – the patronising swine.

The viewer is then treated to a good-natured barman who tells Pauline that English people 'worry too much about time', reinforcing the stereotype of the lazy Irish dosser without a care in the world. Enter Sean, the town drunk, dour and spoiling for a fight. He spills a pint over Pauline, then insults her and leers at her in equal measure. 'We have to be thankful for small mercies – he didn't get violent', the barman tells Mark. *EastEnders* should be thankful the viewers didn't get violent – violently ill after being fed so much horse manure.

Whatever about the above screenplay being enough to

annoy the 'purists', there is one kind of individual who is guaranteed never to be forgiven for painting Mother Ireland anything but the colour of Finian's Rainbow. And he is . . . the treacherous author.

THE TREACHEROUS AUTHOR – Wilde's maxim: 'that the only thing worse than being written about is not being written about' doesn't hold much water in the Irish literary world. Insiders are always punished far more severely than outsiders when they dare to write realistic portrayals of Ireland. 'Realistic', of course, normally means describing an Ireland with a healthy appetite for sex.

James Joyce and **John McGahern** were both great men for the auto-eroticism, the former with Molly Bloom's hanky and the latter with a sock in the night. Both men scandalised Catholic Ireland and weren't let forget it.

JM Synge was another one for upsetting the potato cart. His plays, *In The Shadow of the Glen* and *The Playboy of the Western World* were denounced for suggesting that an arranged marriage could be unhappy or that an Irishman would boast about killing his father. In the case of the former, Arthur Griffiths, Padraig Pearse and almost the entire Nationalist Movement were outraged that the peasantry should be portrayed exactly as they were – lusting, bitter, murderous – just like the rest of the human race.

James Joyce and John McGahern were both great men for the auto-eroticism, the former with Molly Bloom's hanky and the latter with a sock in the night.

Frank McCourt, too, suffered at the hands of Limerick's outraged citizenry for portraying that fine city as a miserable rain-sodden slum where young lads subsist on chips, are forced to empty piss-pots in the street, and abuse themselves manually in front of bemused (and flattered?) sheep.

Then there's **Roddy Doyle** – a man Literary Ireland hasn't made its mind up about. He has all the credentials to be classified as a Treacherous Author. His comic Barrytown Trilogy and subsequent forays into darker material – *The Family* and *The Woman Who Walked Into Doors* – bear the hallmarks of the hated realist. Chips, World Cup soccer, drunken riding on the bonnet of a car ('dare's a good girl, Sharon'), depressed Northside suburbs festooned with communal clotheslines, the non-stop use of the word 'shite' – all add up to treachery. However, the bespectacled former teacher has an ace in the hole (if you'll pardon that scatological expression) – the rest of the world thinks he's great. So great that they gave him the Booker Prize and have turned his books into movies. This is where it gets confusing. Is it OK to like Doyle because he's Irish and everybody loves his view of Ireland? Or should he be shunned for turning a grubby mirror back on us?

If it's the latter, then consider yourself shunned, **Mr Fionn Davenport**.

THE HOMEGROWN TOUR GUIDE – The splendidly named Mr Davenport is the Dublin-born co-author of the *Lonely Planet* guidebooks, renowned for their honest, hard-hitting advice to travellers. In January 2006 the seventh Irish edition was torn asunder (literally, in

Bundoran) for training both barrels on our tourism industry. Amongst other things, it warned tourists that their wallet would be hit hard in Ireland and that anyone who can overcharge usually does.

It also criticised the country's unimaginative approach to its own international reputation, which it claimed still relies on the old Emerald Isle blarney. Davenport also decided that Dundalk resembled a town that couldn't care less about looking pretty for tourists, while Knock was a village crammed with hawkers looking to cash in on the piety of pilgrims.

On the other hand the book praised Belfast for its restaurants and boutiques, while Cork and Limerick also received kind words. Dublin was lauded for its trendy transformation but slated for 'Temple Barf', with its dreadful restaurants, tourist shops, binge-drinking and urine-soaked streets.

In all, *The Lonely Planet Guide to Ireland 2006* was both sincere and brutal, and although the story-hungry press made much of it in the post-Christmas silly season, many in the media – while whipping up a storm – agreed with it. However, the book left itself open to more criticism due to the amount of errors within its pages. One of the most astounding mistakes was the one that advised visitors to buy the defunct *Evening Press* to see what's on in Dublin. The soccer purists were also annoyed with the book for stating that Ireland had qualified for the World Cup finals twice, instead of three times.

Possibly the angriest man in Ireland was the **Bundoran Town Councillor** who said he wanted the town council to consider taking legal action against the guide for describing Bundoran as one of the country's tackiest holiday resorts.

The same man, incidentally, had threatened to sue Met Éireann the previous November for an inaccurate weather forecast that led to the cancellation of a number of events.

Worst Travel Writer Ever

What Giraldus Cambrensis would have made of the *Lonely Planet* hoo-ha is moot. Being the man responsible for writing a book that encouraged unwanted tourists to come to Ireland and stay for 800 years, he qualifies to be called The Worst Travel Writer Ever.

Giraldus Cambrensis, or Gerald of Wales, was a twelfth-century churchman and the author of seventeen books. He was born in 1145 in Pembrokeshire, South Wales. There was royal blood coursing through his veins and Gerald (Gerry to his mates) was self-described as tall, strikingly handsome, and energetic with good interpersonal skills. Giraldus Cambrensis was, in modern parlance, a dick.

Desperately seeking advancement, he first visited Ireland in 1183 and then in 1185, when he was in attendance on Prince John. After John's return, Gerald stayed until Easter 1186, collecting materials for his two works on Ireland: *The Topography of Ireland* and *The Conquest of Ireland*. The former was completed in 1188 and formed an essential part of the Anglo-Norman propaganda machine.

A good example of Gerald in action can be found in the account of the Archbishop of Canterbury's journey to

Wales to enlist soldiers for the coming crusade. Accompanied by the Chief Justiciar of England and attended by a slender young man of 'delicate features and beetling eyebrows' (Guess who?), the archbishop's words had little effect on the peasantry. That was until he asked Gerald to take up the preaching, which he did in Latin and in French. Although the crowd understood neither language, they were moved to tears by his eloquence and 200 men joined up. It was later remarked that if Gerald had spoken in Welsh EVERYONE would have signed up.

The Topography of Ireland is divided into three parts: the first book describes physical features and fauna; the second the marvels of the country, and the third is devoted to early history, followed by a description of manners and dress.

Gerald sets off at a gallop with the opening line: 'Can any good come from Ireland?' and its all downhill after that as the cleric describes a medieval people that love nothing better than killing each other and buggering horses.

It would take up too much space to describe everything Gerald gets wrong about Ireland and its inhabitants so here's a wee taster:

On the island's features

'This farthest island of the West has Spain parallel to it in the south.'

(That would explain why the Spanish are always fishing in our waters then.)

'Ireland is a country of uneven surface . . . low-lying on all sides and the coast; but further inland it rises up very high to many hills and even high mountains.'

(Evidently he never cut turf in the Bog of Allen or headed up the Dublin Mountains for a romp in the back of a 1982 Ford Cortina.)

'This country more than any other suffers from storms and rains.'

(Okay, we'll grant him that.) *On its animals*

'The crane has such a warm and fiery liver that should it eat iron, it will not let it through undigested.'

(The author has tried this. It actually works – a bit.)

'If you hang a dead Kingfisher by its beak in a dry place, it will change its coat of feathers each year.'

(He also says that if you stick a dead one between your sheets it will impart a pleasant aroma. The author has not tried this.)

'There are no black crows in Ireland . . . or if there are, there's not many.'

(Presumably the black ones were disguised as magpies.)

'Due to the dust of this land being poisonous to reptiles, the boot-thongs here are used as antidotes against poisons. They are a particularly effective remedy when cut up in little pieces and taken with water.'

(Someone might have been pulling his leg here.)

On its marvels

'There is an island in a lake in Munster where no woman or animal of the female sex can set foot without dying.' Also . . . 'There is an island to the west of Connacht where there are no mice. For no mouse is bred there nor does one live if it be brought in. If by chance it be brought, it makes straight for the sea and throws itself in. And if it be prevented, it dies on the spot.'

(Evidently there were mice-breeders in Ireland back then. Presumably for the Mice Races at the Curragh.)

Gerald also tells us that two years before the coming of the English a remarkable fish was found at Carlingford in Ulster which had three gold teeth, 'of about fifty ounces in all'. This fish was seen to 'prefigure the imminent conquest of the country'.

(This might have something to do with the better dental healthcare they have in the North. All the fish in the south have ordinary fillings.)

One of the more telling entries is about a wolf that talked to a priest who was resting overnight in a forest in Meath and then became a human. The priest at first was terrified as he had 'for company only a little boy'.

(Most would imagine it would have been the little boy that might have been feeling a little nervous.)

Speaking of half-human hairy creatures Gerald also describes a woman in the court of the King of Limerick who had 'a beard down to her waist with a crest from her neck down her spine like a one-year-old foal. It was covered in hair'.

(Nothing much has changed in Limerick so.)

However, if she thought she had it bad then she hadn't heard about Gerald's friend in Wicklow who had 'the body of a man but all the extremities of an ox. He had hooves and no hair on his head, but was disfigured with baldness. Here and there he had a little down instead of hair. He had ox eyes and instead of a nose he had two holes to act as nostrils. He could not speak at all, but only low. He came to dinner every day and, using his cleft hooves as hands, placed in his mouth whatever was given to him to eat. The Irish natives of the place secretly killed him in the end in envy and malice.'

(Despite the hooves, downy hair, flat nose and mooing sounds, it never crossed Gerald's mind that the unusual dinner guest might, in fact, have actually been an ox. Albeit a bloody clever one.')

The Welsh cleric then goes on to describe the King of Connacht's white goat that liked to have intercourse with women, and a Parisian lion that was fond of engaging with a woman named Johanna, before telling the reader of the deceitful, wretched ways of the untrustworthy Irish who would cut your head off with an axe as soon as look at you.

Mr. Cambrensis throws in a few miracles as well. While pouring cold water on the myth that **St Patrick** banished the snakes, he writes of how a St Nannan managed to banish all the fleas out of a village in Connacht, and how the equally obscure St Yvor expelled the rats of Ferneginan, County Wexford with a curse, for eating his precious books. As Yvor is purportedly the patron saint of engine drivers, legend has it that the rats all caught the 5.25 pm train to Gorey – where they still live.

There are also 'fugitive bells' and 'fires that never go out in Kildare' (the fire brigade are still too afraid to answer calls there without army protection), a talking cross in Dublin, which once actually did get very cross with a Viking, and a fantastic fanatic from Ferns who could 'predict the future', as Gerald puts it, 'from the past'.

While all of the above is hilarious, the damage to Gerald's reputation as a historian comes not from the balderdash he wrote about rats and fleas but about how the Irish were 'a wild and inhospitable people . . . who live like beasts' and are 'lazy' and 'barbarous', 'neither strong in war nor reliable in peace'. In addition, our ancestors were apparently, in the main, blind, lame or generally maimed. A mess, in other words.

Gerald of Wales was undoubtedly a fantastic story-teller, and had he stuck to writing only his more outlandish fantasies, history might have regarded *The Topography of Ireland* as a kind of prototype *Father Ted* screenplay. However, because he said horrible things about us, he is wildly regarded as the Goebbels of the Anglo–Norman invasion of Ireland and . . . **The Worst Travel Writer In Irish History.**

Seeing as how he only ever visited Cork, Waterford, Arklow, Dublin, Kildare and Athlone, it's hard to disagree with the latter view. On the other hand he did a fair job of summing up those places he actually visited. Have you ever been to Arklow?

INTERESTING FACTS

- Gerald was right about St Patrick and the snakes. Many believe the myth is of Norse and not Irish origin. It may be based on the Norse word for toad-expeller (*Pad-rekr*) and the Irish form of Patricius (Padraig).

- *Fair City, EastEnders* or *Coronation Street* don't qualify to be called SOAPS as they are aired in the evening time and the word 'SOAP' is an acronym for Small Output Afternoon Programme.

- There is a story told (probably untrue) about how the misanthropic actor Danny Kaye perceived Ireland when he got snowbound in Dublin Airport in the 1950s. Stuck in the airport bar with nothing to do but glower into a glass, he was asked by the friendly barman if he planned to stay long in the country. 'Ireland,' spat Kaye, with some venom, 'is the asshole of Europe.' 'Ah, you're just passing through so,' replied the barman.

Worst Guardian Of The Crown Jewels

Ulster King of Arms, Sir Arthur Vicars, was by most accounts a fastidious man of outstanding character; trustworthy, honest, upright and all the other appropriate adjectives. Who better to look after the Irish Crown Jewels on behalf of his King? As it turned out, almost anyone but Sir Arthur, as he was the man who lost them. It's probably safe to say that the theft of the Irish Crown Jewels is no longer the talking point it used to be, but in 1907 the scandal surrounding their disappearance rattled plenty of teacups in the drawing rooms of Dublin and London.

The jewels had been a gift to the Order of St Patrick from King William IV in 1831 and were made up from diamonds belonging to Queen Charlotte. The gems were crafted by Rundell, Bridge and Company of London, and consisted of a badge in the shape of the royal insignia and a star festooned with Brazilian diamonds, rubies and emeralds set in silver. There were also five gold collars. The Order, founded in 1783, was on a par with the lofty Knights of the Garter in England and it was customary for the Grand Master to wear the jewels on state occasions, such as the one planned for 10 July – the visit of new King, Edward VII.

Whether the king would have appreciated being greeted by an old man wearing diamonds and a garter is questionable, as four days before his arrival they were stolen (the jewels, not the old chap or the garter). The king was puce with rage (and gout – he had bad gout) and out for blood, and the unwilling donor he was after was Sir Arthur Vicars. It appeared that the senior herald had been a little cavalier with his security arrangements. The safe that the jewels were normally stored in couldn't fit into the new Office of Arms strongroom in Dublin

171

Castle and so Arthur left them unattended in a nearby library. To make matters worse, the safe's lock hadn't even been tampered with, but was opened with a key.

As has already been pointed out, Arthur was an 'upright' character except in the company of his male friends when he tended to list a little bit. Rumours abounded of drunken parties being held in the castle – Britain's most invincible stronghold in Ireland – and there was even a story that at one of these shindigs Arthur got so drunk that his chums took his key and brought the jewels out of the strongroom. The next morning Vicars woke up wearing them.

No one was laughing on this occasion, least of all Arthur's friend, **Frank Shackleton**, who held the title of Dublin Herald and shared a house with him in Clonskeagh. Shackleton had a reputation for being a cad and was one of the chief suspects for the theft along with his friend Captain Richard H Gorges. The latter, too, was renowned for being a bit light-fingered and had money troubles at the time. The trio were up to their proverbials in the proverbial.

Vicars was stripped of his post as Ulster King of Arms after a Viceregal Commission of Enquiry in 1908 found that he had not exercised 'due vigilance or proper care as the custodian of the regalia'. He retired to Kilmorna House near Listowel, County Kerry and lived out the rest of his days a bitter man protesting his innocence. He died on 14 April 1921, shot by the IRA during the burning of Kilmorna during the War of Independence. In his last testament he condemned the king for scapegoating him and fingered Frank Shackleton as 'the real culprit and thief'.

Many believe that, as Shackleton was the brother of polar explorer and national treasure **Sir Ernest Shackleton**, the matter was 'whitewashed' to spare the latter's blushes. In evidence to the commission, Frank also hinted at the involvement of the Lord Lieutenant's son, which was seen as a veiled threat to cause a scandal. This may be the reason why the commission's report stated conclusively that there was no evidence that Shackleton had stolen the gems – an official 'exoneration' to keep him quiet.

If further proof was needed of Frank's dishonesty it arrived in 1913 when he was convicted of fraud. Two years later his delightful friend Captain Gorges was jailed for the manslaughter of a policeman. Frank passed away under an assumed name in 1941 while Gorges died sometime in the 1950s.

Despite the best efforts of Scotland Yard, Sherlock Holmes, Hong Kong Fooey, the Viceregal Commission of Enquiry and a three-week Garda search of the Dublin Mountains in 1983, the €5m jewels have never been found. Their fate remains a subject of wild speculation. Apart from the 1983 hunt, which was ordered after Gardaí 'received information' (as they like to say) from someone on his deathbed, and a couple of practical jokes, the most intriguing footnote to the affair was written in 1976.

On 1 June of that year, the Irish Government revealed the existence of a 1927 memorandum stating that the jewels were for sale and could be bought for '£2,000 or £3,000'.

Did they refuse to buy them back? Let the conspiracy theories begin.

Best Excuse For Breaking Into Jail

While there is no evidence that the aforementioned Shackleton and Gorges ever attempted to break out of jail during their incarcerations, history will remember one Corkman who tried to do the exact opposite.

In the summer of 2006, a Cork District Court Judge asked if he was hearing things correctly when told that a member of the public had tried to stage a reverse jail break at the city's prison. Prison officers had been amazed to witness the 21-year-old man emerging out of the darkness having climbed the seven-metre outer wall of Rathmore Road. The 'reverse fugitive' – let's call him Ford Harrison – was about to scale the inner wall (he had a ladder, so don't be too impressed) when the officers caught up with him.

When asked why he was attempting to break into jail in the middle of the night, Harrison replied that he was taking a shortcut home. He was walking by the prison at 2 am, he told the wide-eyed warders, when he found the ladder up against the wall and decided to climb into the prison to shave some time off the journey. (In fairness, taxis are hard to come by outside a prison at two in the morning. Not much call for them.)

The court also heard that Harrison was being sought by the police about an earlier incident at the time he decided to make his daring non-escape into prison. This remarkable coincidence wasn't lost on the judge, who informed the young man that if he misbehaved again he wouldn't need a ladder to get back into the jail.

Ford Harrison was fined for being drunk and given a suspended sentence for trespassing. His was undoubtedly The Best Excuse for Breaking Into Jail, giving rise to The Best Excuse For Arriving Home Late From The Pub.

Politest
and Rudest

Politest Bank Robber

The following is not intended to influence any young person reading this who may be considering embarking on a life of crime. It's not big or clever to scare people and steal money. So Just Say No! Or is that drugs? Anyway, generally speaking, bank robbers like to:

A: Threaten violence.

B: Curse a lot.

C: Not get caught.

D: Do all of the above at the same time.

This is the rule of thumb for the career criminal. 'In – Shout – Rob – Out'. Couldn't be simpler. Not for Trinity College graduate, **Andrew Flood**, though. (We've changed his name on the grounds that he might have gone straight by now). He was dubbed Ireland's Politest Bank Robber when he caught the public's imagination in November 2005. The disarming robber, who had a diploma in journalism, a degree in philosophy and a masters in psychoanalytic studies, never once resorted to violence or foul language during a six-month spree which netted him €50,000.

During his trial, the court heard how Flood would enter banks in various guises – as a builder or a courier – and would patiently wait in the queue until it was his turn to be 'served'. With a newspaper (probably *The Irish Times*) folded over his hand to conceal an imitation handgun, he would then approach the counter where he would say something along the lines of: 'Please excuse me, ma'am, but I'm here to rob the bank.' He would then show the gun to the stunned teller and ask them to put money in a bag. Sometimes he never spoke a word – he just showed the gun and gave his bag to the teller. (We've all had those days, when you just don't feel like talking.)

It was all very polite, and possibly a bit boring as bank jobs go, but the general consensus seemed to be that it was a far more civilised way to do this kind of dirty business. Flood 'performed' on thirteen occasions before he was caught (the guards said he was extremely co-operative after his arrest). He was given four years in jail – a sentence which many considered too lenient, considering the amount of banks he'd politely robbed with a firearm, albeit an imitation one. The philosophy student probably emitted a

. . . he would then approach the counter where he would say something along the lines of: 'Please excuse me, ma'am, but I'm here to rob the bank.'

little sigh of relief after getting off so lightly.

However, six months later the Court of Criminal Appeal announced it was doing a little 'daylight robbery' of its own and doubled Flood's time in prison on the grounds of 'undue leniency' – a heist that would have had even 'Raffles, the Gentleman Thief' cursing like a docker.

Rudest Joke About A Politician

Whatever about bank robbers like Andrew Flood refraining from turning the air blue, you can always rely on the rugby fraternity to use a few ripe words here and there.

In March 2005 the nation was shocked to learn that a rugby player had cracked a sexy joke about the then Tánaiste, **Mary Harney**. You can decide which part of that last sentence is hardest to believe: the nation being shocked that a rugby type would tell a blue story or that someone could use the words 'sexy', 'Mary' and 'Harney' in the same line. That aside, Lansdowne Rugby Club made a grovelling apology to the PD leader after a former coach made a reported sex 'jibe' about her in a corporate lunch address. The lunch, held before Ireland's tie with France in the Six Nations tournament, was attended by 250 corporate types and their clients. According to the *Evening Herald* the speech, which was peppered with blue jokes, left the sensitive souls present gasping in disbelief. The paper went on to report that one businessman present said he was 'shocked' and that the comments had really 'crossed the line'. Another person equally 'shocked' was Fine Gael's Transport spokesperson **Olivia Mitchell** who said the sex jibe was 'so beneath contempt'. All the other papers picked up on the story and by the end of the week the comments had been dissected and analysed to such an extent that the whole nation had gone into 'SHOCK!!!!'. Whatever about the rude comments, the biggest joke of them all was delivered by Junior Foreign Affairs Minister **Conor Lenihan** when he called for (get this) 'more respect' for politicians. The clown.

So what was this joke that caused such a rumpus? Incredibly no newspaper was willing to publish it on the grounds of bad taste. The author, however, has heard it retold from a tolerably reliable source. Unfortunately, the publisher's Moral and Legal Department has ruled that no gratuitous references to Ms Harney's voluptuousness, sexuality etc may be reprinted in this book. As such, you'll have to speculate as to what was allegedly said.

Here's an observation though: Harney may be curvaceous but Mr Rugby Joke proved there are bigger tits out there.

Now let us zip along over to Mayo and to either the Rudest or Most Honest Man of Them All – Austin Francis O'Malley.

Rudest Politician

Defiant councillor, Austin Francis O'Malley was made of sterner stuff than the Old Boys of Lansdowne Road. The Mayoman caused his own kerfuffle in the same month when he told the *Irish Independent* that he stood over his remark calling on Mary Harney to 'get her fat finger out'. The Fine Gael representative made his digital remarks at a meeting of the regional forum of the Health Service Executive in Galway.

The comment, the paper reported, 'dismayed' many of those attending the forum and prompted chairman Cllr Aidan Colleary to call on Cllr O'Malley to 'withdraw it'. The paper here failed to explain whether he was referring to the comment or Harney's 'fat finger'.

Cllr O'Malley was not for turning and declared that he would 'withdraw nothing', adding prosaically: 'We are on the hind tit for everything in Mayo, whether it is jobs or roads. The health service is pathetic and Minister Harney needs to get her fat finger out and get it sorted.'

Several councillors voiced their disapproval of the comments and repeated the call to 'withdraw it'. Which goes to show that they're not that big on irony in Mayo.

Rudest Hackette

Perhaps if Mary Ellen Synon had just come out and said: 'You're only a crowd of crips', her comments about the Paralympics in the *Sunday Independent* might have barely 'pinged' on the public radar screen – and entered this book under the 'So What?' heading. (Luckily there is no 'So What?' heading in this book as we couldn't be bothered writing one.) However, her excellent way with words ensured that her musings on disabled athletes were never going to be ignored by a furious public.

In 2000 the journalist reinforced her knack for being

very, very annoying when she referred to the participants in the 2000 Paralympics in Sydney as 'the lame and the blind', and also 'cripples' who wobbled their way around tracks in wheelchairs or swam from one end of a pool to the other 'by Braille'. The whole business, while not 'grotesque', was 'perverse', she opined, throwing in a line about Stephen Hawking showing his wisdom by staying out of the three-legged race.

Not that controversy was anything new to Synon. Her right-wing outpourings against travellers, trade unionists, socialists, asylum-seekers and even education for the disadvantaged had consistently raised the hackles of not only the Liberal Left in the Irish media but also the Maureens and Micheáls of Middle Ireland.

The fact that she had a whiny American accent didn't help either (she's from Virginia – the USA one, not the Cavan one). Her championing of capitalism reached its zenith when she failed to come out in support of Susan O'Keeffe, whose revelations about Beef Baron Larry Goodman resulted in the establishment of the first of the major tribunals. When she wrote that she'd be happy to see O'Keeffe in handcuffs, she declared open season on herself.

She also cleverly called for a 32-county Ulster, as a means of fooling Unionists into a United Ireland, and defended the right to bear arms (thankfully not in the same article), quoting the old Charlton Heston line: 'You can take my gun when you prise it from my cold, dead fingers.' An article she wrote in 1996 even prompted the travellers' support group, Pavee Point, to seek advice under Ireland's incitement to hatred laws.

This time, however, she had pushed the nuclear button, and the television shots of Irish Paralympians winning five gold medals and three silvers helped to scatter the fallout far and wide. There were reports that members of the team had burst into tears after hearing her quotes.

The response by the public and the Independent Newspaper Group was both over- and under-whelming. Radio shows were a-babble with outraged listeners and the *Sindo* suffered boycotts, most notably from the Hospitaller Order of St John of God in Shankill, County Dublin, who said the centre was withdrawing its subscription on behalf of its disabled clients. The owner of Dublin's city centre shops, Centra, also withdrew copies of the paper.

The editor of the *Sunday Independent* dithered, first defending the article and then apologising for it. Tony O'Reilly, owner of the 'Indo' Group, was believed to be behind the latter response as, defending the indefensible aside, he and his wife were directors of the Barretstown camp in Kildare for seriously ill children.

In her apology Synon said it was never her intention to 'hurt or demean anyone, certainly not any disabled person. I understand now that I did, and for that I apologise'. She added that she could say this with 'particular personal reason' as she knew 'more about legs that cannot walk and a spine that will not hold' than she was 'prepared to say'. She also admitted that she had judged her choice of words badly.

For some the front page apology was not enough and

one prominent Labour Party councillor called on the Eastern Regional Health Authority and its health boards to suspend advertising with the *Sunday Independent* for six months in protest. Shortly after the apology was published Synon resigned.

By a strange kink of fate the name 'Mary Ellen Synon' is an anagram of 'Nylon my arse, Noel'. It also happens to be an anagram of 'Nelly Myers, anon' which makes even less sense other than it includes the surname of the commentator who subsequently took over as Pot-Stirrer Laureate, Kevin 'Bloody' Myers of *The Irish Times*.

Rudest Hack For Calling People 'Bastards'

In February 2005, *The Irish Times* published a page one apology for an article in which Irishman's Diary regular, Kevin Myers depicted children born to unmarried parents as 'bastards'. In fairness to him he didn't say they shouldn't be competing in international sporting events, but the entire country went Balubas over his comments. It is entirely possible that more people readily admitted to being outraged by Myers' remarks than had ever read any of his columns before, but that is a moot point (as opposed to Synon's argument which was a 'deaf-mute' point).

His extraordinary rant in *The Irish Times* was a follow-up to controversial remarks made by the former head of the University of Limerick, Edward Walsh, to the effect that generous welfare allowances were encouraging underprivileged teenage girls to get pregnant. This, Walsh argued, was leading to social dysfunction and in some cases, criminality.

In a nutshell: Jacinta gets 'up the pole' to avail of the 'mickey money' and gives birth to little Wayne, who eventually becomes a Big Wayne who obliges Melissa in her attempts to get 'up the duff' to avail of the 'mickey money' and so on, with all the attendant problems this brings.

Myers joined in the debate by asking how many girls 'consciously embark upon a career of mothering bastards because it seems a good way of getting money and accommodation from the state?' In a wide-ranging article about benefits to unmarried mothers, the columnist suggested that our welfare system was creating 'benefits-addicted, fatherless families' that would be raised in a culture of personal and economic apathy. It was an argument that had been made many times before and debated between countless radio show callers and taximen. The problem was the use of the word 'bastards' and his description of their mums as 'mothers of bastards', or MoBs for short.

'Ah. You didn't like the term bastard,' Myers wrote. 'No, I didn't think you would. In the welfare-land of Euphemesia, what is the correct term for the offspring of unmarried mothers?'

It appeared that anything other than 'bastard' would be the correct term, judging by the outcry. Myers used the word sixteen times (if you include the acronyms, MoBs and FoBs) in a calculated way that was designed to provoke an extreme reaction. In fact, though his basic argument may, or may not, have been flawed and its delivery a bit immature, Myers was entitled to pen his concern for the future good of society and those 'impressionable' young women in question – a fact passed over by many of his detractors.

He claimed that the benefits system for unmarried mothers was creating a long-term time bomb by 'bribing . . . the unmotivated, the confused, the backward, the lazy into making the worst career decision of their young lives'. He also added that 'we all agree it is mad to bribe impressionable young women into a life of MoBbery, which is crushingly limiting, with little sense of achievement or personal ambition, and no career to speak of, other – that is – from cash-crop whelping'.

Obviously tarring every unmarried mother (who claims the benefits she is entitled to) as an MoB is grossly offensive and well off the mark but then Myers has always liked to stun his readers (and non-readers) with a little left-of-field jiggery pokery. In an article on the death of his beloved cat he wrote how he (the cat that is, not Myers) loved to 'lick his scrummy'(and it was the cat's scrummy, not Myers', that got licked, lest there be any mistake about it). Anyone who can get away with using a porno term to describe a

> **(Myers) claimed that the benefits system for unmarried mothers was creating a long-term time bomb by 'bribing . . . the unmotivated, the confused, the backward, the lazy into making the worst career decision of their young lives'.**

pussycat grooming itself deserves to be lauded as a genius. Describing babies as bastards is not so clever though.

The Irish Times described itself as very, very sorry for any offence caused and Myers himself admitted his choice of words had lost him the argument. He also claimed that he hadn't intended to cause offence. (Sixteen bastards in the one column, Kevin? Kevin??!! Hellooo, is there anybody home???? No offence intended? Will you go on out of that . . .)

As Kevin Myers had been deliberately rude about a section of society, he must now take a bow and accept the title of Rudest Hack For Calling People 'Bastards'.

For the record, nowhere in this book will you find cats gratuitously referred to as 'pussy', or dogs as 'bitches'.

Nor will you find a spade being called a 'spade'.

Politest Newspaper Apology

Unlike Kevin Myers, former Taoiseach Garret Fitzgerald never publicly labelled anybody a bastard. He will be remembered for many other things: the Anglo-Irish Agreement and its 'Ulster Says No' reaction from the Reverend Ian Paisley; his intellect; his habit of wearing odd socks; and those remarkable TV duels with Charlie Haughey in the 1980s.

He will also be remembered for the singular 'correction' printed in *The Irish Times* of 29 August 2006.

Garret was always the first to chide himself for being less than humble, but even his most ardent admirers were stunned by the shocking description of himself in a preview of RTÉ's 'Fitzgerald at 80' series, which prompted the following polite clarification: 'Dr Fitzgerald has since pointed out (to *The Irish Times*) that he would never, and did not, on this occasion, use such language. The word he used was 'prig'. The error is regretted.'

The reporter has since been fitted with a hearing aid.

Rudest Description Of A Landlord's Erection

As anyone who has sat through a Wolfe Tones' concert knows, all Irish folk songs are about getting hung by the Redcoats for stealing a loaf of stale bread for the starving children or being transported for failing to tug one's forelock as his honour, the landlord, rolls over your foot with his carriage. The latter, by the by, is the reason why so many of Australia's early Irish settlers were bald and why today that country has the highest sales of Rogaine and wigs in the world. One famous Irish-Australian, Ned Kelly, was so ashamed of his baldness that he rode around with a bucket on his head. He became an outlaw after battering a policeman who mistook him for a letterbox and tried to post a parking fine through the eye-slit while Ned was taking a nap outside the pub. Thereafter he made a considerable fortune out of pretending to be a mailbox – cashing in all the postal orders and ransoming all the orders for adult magazines and inflatable dolls people would stick in his bucket.

Aside from the forelock tugging, another tradition favoured by the landlord classes was the *droit de seigneur* or 'right of the lord'. This 'entitled' the landlord to take the virginity of a young woman tenant the night before she got married – rape in other words. This horrible practice existed in Ireland until the end of the nineteenth century and there are still folk tales told in rural Ireland of the consequences of refusing the landlord his traditional right. There is one story remembered in County Roscommon of a girl who said 'no' to her landlord and was tied, ankles and wrists, to four horses who were then whipped and made race off. Yuch.

One traditional piping tune, 'Corney Is Coming', was believed to be written about **Cornelius O'Brien** (born 1872), a landlord in the Liscannor area of County Clare, who was famed for the tower he had built on the Cliffs of Moher to enforce his *droit de seigneur* and 'entertain' his guests.

Actually there's no evidence that Cornelius – a descendant of Brian Boru and the O'Briens of Bunratty Castle – was a rampant '*seigneur*' at all. In fact, it's now said that he was ahead of his time, believing that the development of tourism on the Cliffs of Moher would benefit the local economy and the poor of the area. In 1853 he built O'Brien's Tower as an observation point for the hundreds of tourists who, even back then, visited the cliffs. It is still the best place from which to view the cliffs as well as the Aran Islands, Galway Bay, The Twelve Pins, the Maum Turk Mountains and Loop Head.

Lewis Topographical Dictionary, 1837 refers to his home at Birchfield as:

The residence of Cornelius O'Brien who has much improved his estate and the condition of his tenantry by the erection of neat slated cottages and farm buildings and by other judicious arrangements; a holy well dedicated to St Bridget and much resorted to by the peasantry, which, at Mr. O'Brien's expense, has been surrounded by tasteful plantations and rustic seats.

Unlike other rack-renting landlords in County Clare, O'Brien is described as a model landlord (if such a thing is not an oxymoron) and was even accused of favouring his own tenants when allocating famine relief work as a member of the Liscannor Famine Relief Committee. His work for the poor earned him this obituary in the Clare Journal of 1853:

As a landlord, no man was held in greater love and esteem by his tenantry. They clung to him in many a well-fought field of contention and carried him triumphant through every contest.

Typically, Cornelius is remembered for none of the above, just for the alleged, still unsubstantiated, *droit*.

To this day the column on his grave in St Bridget's Well Cemetery is referred to as 'Cornelius O'Brien's Last Erection'. How rude is that?

INTERESTING FACT

- Cornelius was also a Member of Parliament for the region and was recalled, on his death, by Lord Palmerston as 'the best Irish MP we ever had. He didn't open his mouth in 20 years'.

Youngest and Oldest

Youngest Taoiseach To Hold Office

That would be Bartholomew Ahern (as if you didn't know). Bertie was elected to the office in 1997 at the sprightly age of 45. He first became involved in politics at the age of 14 when he shinned up lampposts to hang by-election posters for Fianna Fáil. You could say that Charlie Haughey got him up the pole/poll at an early age but that would just drag us back into the previous 'Rudest' section.

Bertie – who likes the youthful pursuits of cooking, drinking Bass, watching soccer, mispronouncing 'tings', going to Westlife gigs – was a full ten years junior to **Eamon de Valera** when he became the first person to use the title Taoiseach in 1937. Prior to this, the post of Prime Minister had been called Príomh Aire or President of the Executive Council. The first Príomh Aire was Cathal Brugha who relinquished his role to de Valera in 1919. Despite the use of the word 'President' the position was not that of a head of state.

Edward George de Valera was the son of a Spanish-Cuban dad, Juan Vivion de Valera, and Irish mother, Catherine Coll de Valera Wheelwright, and was born in New York city in 1882. Some scholars believe that he may have been illegitimate. Whether Kevin Myers would have called him a bastard to his face is a matter purely for conjecture and belongs in the previous section to which we keep returning at an alarming rate.

In 1885, following the death of his sculptor father, de Valera's uncle Ned brought him over to County Limerick where he was raised by his grandmother, Elizabeth Coll, along with her son, Patrick, and her daughter, Hannie. His mother later remarried but young de Valera wasn't sent back to the States. Luckily for him (and unluckily for Michael Collins) it was this American connection that saved his skin during the execution of the leaders of 1916. It was not his citizenship that protected him, as many believe, but a protracted legal consultation over whether he actually had citizenship and what the Americans would do if the British shot him. As the latter prevaricated the public mood in Ireland turned angry and the executions were halted, thus leaving him 'unplugged' for his time spent leading the rebels in Boland's Mills.

De Valera liked titles and apart from Taoiseach, Príomh Aire, President of the Executive Council, Chancellor of the National University of Ireland, President of the

Assembly at the League of Nations (1938) he was also the
. . . Oldest President To Hold Office.

Oldest President To Hold Office

Eamon de Valera was the oldest person to hold the presidency when, at the age of 76, he wobbled up the steps of Áras an Uachtaráin in 1959. When he shuffled out again in 1973 after his second term had ended he was 91, blind and the oldest head of state of any country in the world. He has the unusual distinction of being not only the Oldest President but also the . . . Youngest President To Hold Office.

Youngest President To Hold Office

Eamon de Valera was the first President of the Republic and not Douglas Hyde, as other less scholarly books than this insist. Hyde was 78 years old when he was elected by all-party agreement in 1938. He served until 1945 and was succeeded by Sean T O'Kelly (63) who then handed the reigns over to de Valera.

This was the second time that the Long Fellow had been head of the Irish State. In 1921 he had himself constitutionally upgraded from President of Dáil Éireann (Príomh Aire/Prime Minister) to full President of the Republic with all the bells and whistles attached. As Dev was 39 at the time he remains the Youngest President To Hold Office.

He stood down as president during the Dáil Treaty debates and the office of President of The Republic was abolished in 1922, three months after the death of Arthur Griffiths in August 1922. WT Cosgrave was the last person to hold the title.

In 1937 de Valera constituted his new Irish Constitution or Bunreacht na hÉireann, which paved the way for Douglas Hyde to become the first President since the foundation of the Free State. Being so advanced in years the 'fine and scholarly old gentleman', as FD Roosevelt once called him, was bound to have health problems. In 1940 he survived a huge stroke, but remained paralysed and confined to a wheelchair.

This wasn't the only stroke Hyde had while in the Áras, if the rumour mill of the time was to be believed. His incapacitation led him to retire from public view and in time speculation mounted that he had become senile and exceptionally randy. The object of his lust, the gossipmongers claimed, was his entire female household staff and, in particular, his young nurse. The rumours were all untrue. He remained mentally alert and a gentleman to his fingertips until the end.

If they had been true, one wonders what Mary Ellen Synon would have said about that kind of sporting activity taking place in a wheelchair.

INTERESTING FACTS

- President Cearbhall Ó Dálaigh was a fervent Irish language enthusiast and once gave a press conference to international journalists 'as Gaeilge'. On another occasion, whilst on a state visit, he opted to speak every major European language except for English.

- The last King of Ireland was George VI (Elizabeth II's father), who although unofficially dethroned by Hyde in 1937, was legally the Irish monarch until 1949. The first king was Henry I – who was in fact Henry VIII. Confused? The Irish Parliament created the Kingdom of Ireland and the title King of Ireland in 1541 to replace the Lordship of Ireland, which had existed since 1171, two years after the first Norman invasion. This meant that from then on whoever was on the throne in England was also King of Ireland. The first holder of the title, therefore, was King Henry VIII. However, since there had never been a King Henry of Ireland before, he was also known officially as King Henry I of Ireland.

  The first Lord of Ireland was Prince Henry I (1171–1189). He later ruled England as Henry II. (Got all that?)

- The first High King of Ireland according to the *Annals of the Four Masters* was the Firbolg chieftain, Slaine. The last Gaelic High King was Edward Bruce (1274–1318) who had invaded Ireland to open a second front for his brother, Robert the Bruce, who was at war with England in Scotland. He was 41 when he assumed the title and died three years later.

- The ancient Irish devotion to Mary meant that the first two female presidents had to bear the same name. Apart from this similarity, Mrs McAleese and Mrs Robinson were also both 46 years of age when they took office (the former in 1997 and the latter in 1990).

Oldest Traffic Light

According to legend Dublin's northside is home to the country's Oldest Traffic Light. Situated beside what used to be the Renault garage on the Clontarf Road, the light was installed in 1893 and even had its own operator to move the candle from the red chamber to the green chamber when required. As there was only one motorist on the road at the time – **Mr Fergus Mitchell** was the first man to own a car in Ireland – the traffic light was placed, conveniently, outside his house.

Whether Mr Mitchell ever had a prang in his jalopy is not recorded, but it is safe to say that he was not responsible for the World's First Car Fatality. This, sadly, occurred in Parsontown, County Offaly on 31 August 1869. The victim was renowned artist, naturalist, astronomer and microscopist **Mary Ward**. She and her husband were passengers in a home-made steam-powered car which took a jolt at the corner of Cumberland Street and Oxmantown Mall at 8.30 pm, throwing her off the vehicle and under its wheel. She died almost instantly.

Mary held many distinctions as an artist and scientist and was the first woman to write and have published a book on the microscope, in spite of the chauvinism of the age. She now has the further distinction of being as famous for her death as she was for her achievements in life. Her accident also hastened the demise of the steam-powered car, which was already on its knees as a result of the Locomotive (Red Flag) Act of 1865, which limited speeds to 'four miles an hour in the country and two miles an hour in the town'. Under the Act drivers also had to employ a man with a red flag or lantern who would walk '60 yards in front of each vehicle' warning horse riders of his master's approach.

The Oldest Case of Road Rage was recorded in early 1893 when the very last 'Red Flag' man tried to ram his flagpole up the backside of a corporation worker who was making him redundant by installing the first (real) traffic light on the Clontarf Road.

INTERESTING FACT

- Leitrim, historically the poor relation in Ireland's family of counties, finally got its first set of traffic lights in 2003 at the Leitrim Road junction in the bustling metropolis of Carrick-on-Shannon. The acting director of services with Leitrim County Council told reporters that there had been problems at 'peak times'.

Oldest Shop in Dublin

Thomas Reads of Parliament Street could also be catalogued under the heading Best Place To Trim A Housefly's Whiskers, but it is marginally more famous for being Dublin's Oldest Shop. The cutlers business first started making knives, duelling swords and halberds (a long shaft with an axe blade and a pick, topped by a spearhead) in 1670 on Blind Quay, moving to Crane Lane in 1750 and on to its present location when the Wide Street Commissioners built Parliament Street.

Reads was famous for its glass-fronted cabinets and framed 'Ye Olde Licence' to sell the aforementioned nasty articles. The business has also been mentioned in many literary works including James Joyce's *Ulysses* and Charles Lever's infinitely more famous novel *Handy Andy* about a useful manservant.

Among the unique items on display were the World's Smallest Working Scissors, said to be able to 'trim a housefly's whiskers'. Quite why you would want to do the latter is still a matter for debate. Apparently Dublin's more fashionable bluebottles wouldn't be seen dead anywhere else but in Reads' window.

Another item of note was The World's Biggest Penknife, which had 576 blades – and was presumably made for The World's Biggest Boy Scout.

The last Read – John Read Cowle – sold up in 1989 and although the place is still listed as Dublin's Oldest Shop in the guidebooks, it is now just a shuttered-up shell attached to a pub which also bears the same name. Still, at least tourists visiting the hostelry can boast they got 'half cut in half a cutlers'.

Old though it may be, Reads can't hold a candle to the city's most ancient business – Rathbornes, who can boast of being the Oldest Manufacturers in Ireland and Best Place For Stocking Up On Belgian Candles.

Set up on Winetavern Street in 1488 by John Rathborne from Cheshire, the World's Oldest Candlemakers (so they claim) remained in the hands of the Rathborne family and their descendants until just after the First World War, when the advent of electrification appeared to spell the end for the candle business.

Business tapered off in the holy 1960s when most candles were being bought only for churches and for special occasions like Christmas and blackouts, but picked up again when candles came back into fashion in the 1980s and 1990s. It is estimated that 95% of candles sold in Ireland are bought by women. The other 5% are, presumably, bought by priests as Rathbornes is still the biggest supplier of Church candles in the country.

What then could be more apt than Ireland's oldest company being awarded the contract to make the 1.3 million 'Millennium' candles distributed with a special scroll to every Irish home to celebrate Jesus' 2000th birthday? Rathbornes were delighted when the Fianna Fáil-led government gave the company the nod to light up the nation's windows on New Year's Eve in 1999.

There was, however, one considerable drawback – the order for the 'Last Light Project' came too late for the firm to make all the candles itself. Incredibly, it was mid-October before the National Millennium Committee got around to asking the company to fill the order – leaving only two months to get the job done. As a result, Rathbornes had no other choice but to subcontract to two companies, one in Germany and one in Belgium. The bright side for the Dublin firm was that they got to put their name on the finished product.

Actually, 1999 was a very good year for the firm as the soaring candle sales for the millennium were sparked not just by people buying them for New Year ceremonies but also by others stockpiling in case the Y2K bug knocked out the country's electricity (which it didn't).

It wasn't such a good year, however, for Fianna Fáil **Minister of State Seamus Brennan**. The candles weren't the only millennium project to suffer from his committee's lack of urgency, and his political career will perhaps be best remembered for his tenure as Minister in Charge of the . . . Longest Millennium Celebration Ever.

Longest, Shortest and Tallest

Longest Millenium Celebration Ever

This countywide celebration continued for at least three years (or is still in full swing depending on what project you consider the centrepiece of the government's festivities). If the erection of **The Spire** in O'Connell Street was Ireland's ultimate salute to the new Millennium, then bear in mind that it took three years and several kilometres of red tape to build. The year 2000 was almost over before the replacement for Nelson's Pillar even got past the environmental impact stage and it wasn't until January 2003 that an underwhelmed populace first marvelled at the World's Biggest Needle Exchange Programme (the taxpayer's part of the exchange being IR£4m (€5m)). Designed by an English architect, this 120 m spike, which is 3 m wide at the base and has a 15 cm beacon at its tip, is the city's second least favourite monument. The least favourite was the Anna Livia fountain on O'Connell Street (known affectionately as the 'Floozy in the Jacuzzi'), which was subjected to various indignities over the years, including having her bath regularly filled up with washing-up liquid. She was removed in 2001 to make way for the Spire.

If the fulcrum of your millennium celebration was to be the release of the Millennium Song by former Boyzone singer **Ronan Keating**, then your party is still in full swing. Mr Keating – who was on the Millennium Committee – offered to write a song to raise money for charity. However, after penning the words to 'Make The Change' he ran out of time and couldn't get it produced. However, there's still time to rework it for the next millennium. While Keating's project remains a work-in-progress many of the 2,400 national and local projects that were eventually completed should surely have been considered 'better never than late'.

One millenium moment of madness that had no concept of time at all was the 'Chime In The Slime'. This illuminated clock in the Liffey was designed to count down to 2000, but as no one could read it, it was quietly removed long before the celebrations began.

Then there was the Liffey Boardwalk (phase one of which finally opened on 18 December 2000). This was to coincide with the romantically titled 'Liffey of Lights', an ambitious plan where every major bridge across the river would be lit up against the night sky. The problem was that the many tourists who thronged the city merely saw exactly how dirty the Liffey really was. The Liffey of Durex Lites, if you will.

The People's Millennium Forests – which sound more like the type of place where dissidents were shot in Soviet Russia – were another seemingly visionary way to spend the allotted IR£33m (€42m). Under this sylvan scheme, more than 1.2 million native trees were planted in fourteen forests. The plan was that one tree – the majority of which were oaks – would be planted in the name of each household in the country. Every householder would then get a map pinpointing exactly where their tree was planted. What **Minister Brennan** and his band of intrepid woodsmen neglected to tell a delighted public at the time was that by 2001 a quarter of the trees would have died, been walked on or been chopped down. As a result, by the end of 2005 only 1 in 10 families would still have a tree to hug.

. . . the 'postponement' of Millennium 2000AD led to (Deputy Brennan's) crucifixion at the hands of his opponents in the Dáil Chamber during a gory Question Time.

Although Deputy Brennan was not personally responsible for all the delays, the 'postponement' of Millennium 2000AD led to his own crucifixion at the hands of his opponents in the Dáil Chamber during a gory Question Time.

'What happened,' wondered Labour's Pat Rabbitte, laying out his hammer and nails on the front bench, 'did the millennium creep up on you?'

A disaster that wouldn't have happened to The World's Biggest Boy Scout with The World's Biggest Penknife. 'Be Prepared' etc and so forth.

INTERESTING FACTS

- Rathbornes can also claim the title of Oldest Best-Travelled Business in Dublin. It moved three times: firstly from Winetavern Street to Stoneybatter in 1600 and then on to East Wall in 1925. From there the firm headed into the Wild West of Blanchardstown, touching the final point on the Dublin compass – South, North, East and West.

- Nelson's Pillar was designed by William Wilkins of Norwich and the statue was sculpted by Irish sculptor, Thomas Kirk, R.H.A. It cost £6,856 to build and was erected in 1808.

- The largest cake ever baked in the capital weighed 86 kg and was made to celebrate the 1988 Dublin City Millennium. It was thrown out of the Mansion House in 1991 but eventually returned in 2004 disguised as Cllr Royston Brady.

Longest Funeral Cortège

The funeral of Michael John Collins (1890–1922) was the largest the country had ever seen. The revolutionary leader drew hundreds of thousands of mourners and the world's media to Dublin after he was mortally wounded during an ambush at Béal na Bláth on 22 August 1922. In his 32 years of life, he served as Minister for Finance, Director of Intelligence for the IRA, Príomh Aire of the Provisional Government, Commander-in-Chief of the National Army and negotiated a treaty with Britain. His loss to the nascent Free State was immense and his funeral was commensurate with his legendary status.

Commander-in-Chief of the Free State army, General Richard Mulcahy, gave the oration at Glasnevin Cemetery and called his comrade 'the fallen leader, a great hero and a great legend'. Even that old sour puss, Ulster Unionist leader James Craig described it as 'a terrible loss'. Had he known that Collins was organising a border campaign at the time of his death he might have kept his gob shut.

Figures for the amount of people who turned out to pay their respects differ. The titles at the end of **Neil Jordan's** epic movie *Michael Collins* declare that half a million people flooded the streets. On the other hand the *Irish Independent* of the day put the number at 300,000. Using a compromise figure of 400,000 it is possible to calculate, with 100% accuracy, the true length of the cortège, which the paper described as the 'Greatest pageant of sorrow ever seen in Dublin: a cortège three miles long.' As Glasnevin Cemetery was (and still is) just short of 2.5 miles from the city centre, this length sounds a bit bogus. If we allow for the 18 inches of personal space we all need to feel comfortable and an average width of 10 inches for each mourner, multiplied by the compromise figure of 400,000 we arrive at a total of almost 177 miles. QED. (If you want to check this again in metric: Glasnevin Cemetery is about 4 km from the city centre and the cortège works out as (45 cm + 25 cm) x 400,000 = 280 km.)

That's almost one twenty-third the length of the coastline of Ireland or nearly its entire width from coast to coast (304 km). Incidentally, a resident of Ireland is never more than 100 km away from the coast, but eats a mere 16 kg of seafood per year, and Leitrim has Ireland's shortest coastline – 3 km of beach.

But back to *Michael Collins*. Jordan shot the Bloody Sunday scenes for this biopic at the home of Bray Wanderers Football Club, replacing Croke Park with the Carlisle Grounds. And talking of Bray – it was also the birthplace of Ireland's . . . Longest Serving Altar Boy.

Longest Serving Altar Boy

Exactly one year after Collins had served with Pearse and Connolly in the GPO during the Easter Rising, Tommy Kinsella began serving Mass in the Church of the Holy Redeemer, Bray. Pious Tommy continued to do so in the same church for 81 years until his death in 1999. He may even have formed part of the Longest Funeral Cortège at Collins' funeral.

Collins, as mentioned above, served in the GPO under James Connolly who inspired the . . . Longest Play Ever.

Longest Play Ever

Agatha Christie's *The Mousetrap* may be the world's longest-running play (first performance in London in 1952 and still being staged), but two Irish playwrights have the distinction of being the authors of the World's Longest Play. Titled *The Non-Stop Connolly Show*, the play was first staged at Liberty Hall in Dublin at Easter 1975. It was sponsored by the ITGWU and co-directed by *My Left Foot* (1989) director Jim Sheridan. Through various readings it related the life and work of the enigmatic socialist leader of the Citizen's Army from boyhood to execution – for a bum-numbing twenty-six hours. The play made it into book form and has be-numbed many a cultured buttock from London to New York. It may have been responsible for the Longest Period Of Time Holding On To One's Wee And Staying Awake, but nobody has come forward to claim that particular record.

INTERESTING FACTS

- While Liam Neeson's performance as Michael Collins in the Jordan film is creditable and Brendan Gleeson's in *The Treaty* (1991) is definitive, there is one other major Hollywood star who had a go at portraying the Big Fellow on the silver screen. David Niven, who usually plays the definitive English gentleman, took the main role in *Beloved Enemy* (1936).

Bewildering casting aside, one interesting deviation from the facts was that while Collins did get shot in both real life and this movie, in the latter he actually survived.

• Glasnevin cemetery, originally called Prospect Cemetery, was opened in February 1832 and is also the last resting place of Parnell and O'Connell amongst other great patriots.

Longest Running Chat Show Host

RTÉ's *The Late Late Show* was first broadcast on Friday 6 July 1962 at 11.20 pm and still plagues the airwaves with its mixture of innuendo, live sacrifices and repeated interviews with Daniel O'Donnell. **Gay Byrne** who hosted the weekly 'shockorama' until 1999 is credited with being the Longest Serving Television Host In The World – but he's not.

The chap holding that record goes by the name of Don Francisco. Don's real name is **Mario Kreutzberger** (not of the Roscommon Kreutzbergers) and since 1962 he has been the host of *Sábado Gigante* (yes, you've guessed correctly, it means Gigantic Saturday) – a Chilean blend of game and variety show. Don/Mario says the only way he'll stop doing it is when he's dead.

So Gaybo is the Second Longest Serving Television Host in the World then? Nope, that would be **Bob**

Baxter of *The Price Is Right*, who has been MC on the show since it began 34 years ago in 1972.

Don't bother reaching for your abacus, Gaybo may have started on *The Late Late Show* in 1962 and ended in 1999, but he didn't spend 37 consecutive years corrupting the nation – only 29. Not many people remember this, but Uncle Gabriel took an entire season off (1968/69) quitting to work for the BBC. *The Late Late Show* was given to satirical journalist **Frank Hall**, but Byrne was ultimately enticed back. This means that his longest unbroken stint was from September 1969 to May 1999. This monumental run of 29 years and nine months places him third in the Television Host Table.

Gaybo is, however, the World's Longest Serving Chat Show Host, pipping the late, late Johnny Carson of the *Tonight Show* by just over a month. Johnny broadcast from October 1962 to 1992 – a period of 29 years, seven months and twenty-one days.

INTERESTING FACT

- The distinctive, stomping theme tune to *The Late Late Show* ('DAH-DAH DE DE DE DAH-DAH, DAH-DAH DE DE DE DAH-DAH') was an instrumental version of Chris Andrews' 1965 Number 17 UK hit, 'To Whom It Concerns'. His biggest hit remains 'Yesterday Man', which he is definitely not. Chris is still touring, and the Germans wet themselves at the mention of his name.

Shortest Irishman

The Shortest Irishman in history was the renowned Raymond O'Brien, who popped his clogs in 1795. He was 0.6 m tall, which must have been great for looking up women's skirts but a right pain while attending sporting events. Another chap who was a great sports fan but would have destroyed his back trying to look up skirts was the . . . Tallest Irishman, Patrick O'Brien.

Tallest Irishman

Patrick Cotter O'Brien (1760–1806) was born in Kinsale, County Cork, and measured 2.46 m. He was also the Tallest Man In The World during his lifetime.

When Patrick Cotter was 18 and working as a brickie, he was 'discovered' by a travelling showman who brought him to England to star in his Freak of Nature show (or if that didn't work out, get him building the world's tallest building). Patrick added the stage name 'O'Brien' to give himself a more Celtic air. For the next 25 years he toured England and could command fees of up to 2s for private performances in front of 'the quality'. His act was dependent on the element of surprise and so when he wasn't scaring the bejayzus out of the bewigged upper crust of England, he would stay out of sight in his cramped quarters. He inevitably suffered health problems and would occasionally go to take the air in Epping Forest at night, which caused a few Highwaymen to soil their underpants and decide to change their ways.

Before his death in Bristol (where he is still referred to

as the 'Bristol Giant') he gave instructions that his corpse be protected from grave-snatchers. It took fourteen pallbearers to lower his casket into a vault cut 4 m into solid rock, with massive iron bars cemented into the walls. He still rests there today and his huge boots are on display at Kinsale Museum in County Cork.

Mercifully, he never met and fell in love with the . . . Shortest Irishwoman.

Shortest Irishwoman

Meathwoman Bridget Una McMahon (1770–1823) measured 23 cm in height. Due to an unfortunate incident when a pet parakeet attempted to mate her, she lived her entire life hidden away in a specially adapted shoebox, surviving on a diet of nuts and cheese. In 1823, timid, terrified Bridget was persuaded by her family to come out and celebrate her 53rd birthday. Sadly after consuming three egg cups of beer she walked into a mousetrap. She is buried in Trim graveyard, County Meath.

INTERESTING FACT

- The average height of an Irish male is 1.7 m (5 feet 7 inches).

Shortest Irish Blues Song About The Dole

(E major)

'Woke up this morning,

Rolled over,

Went back to sleep.'

– Dick Rafferty and The Sluice Juice Self-Aid, May 1986

Longest Period Spent Dancing For World Peace

Approximately 20 years, give or take a week or two.

In 2003 one of the great revelations of modern times occurred. Millions of people sitting in their homes suddenly discovered that the end of the world was at hand. A powerful interpreter of the prophets brought their attention to this hitherto fore little known fact. He was, naturally enough, from County Kerry. Knockeenahone, Scartaglin, to be exact. On 20 July of that year **Father Cornelius Neil Horan** ran onto the track at the British Grand Prix in Silverstone wearing a kilt and waving a banner, with the following command on it: 'Read the Bible. The Bible is always right'. Fr Horan had done a very dangerous thing – encouraging young men to read books while driving the fastest cars on the planet. Imagine the chaotic road-handling while attempting to turn the pages and keep an eye on the road. Standing in the middle of a racetrack is also a bit dangerous and several cars had to swerve to avoid him on the 320 kph Hangar Straight. The safety car was even deployed. Horan was arrested, pleaded guilty to aggravated trespass and was sentenced to two months.

He also performed a similar deed at the 2004 Summer Olympics men's marathon in Athens. Wearing a green waistcoat, red kilt, green knee socks and floppy green tam-o-shanter, he ran onto the course with a placard proclaiming the imminent end of the world. To the consternation of all concerned (except himself) Horan pushed the race leader, Vanderlei de Lima, from Brazil into the spectators. De Lima finished third and was denied, on appeal, a share in a gold medal. Horan, meanwhile, had been carted off by Greek police, had apologised for ruining de Lima's race and was given a 12 months' suspended sentence and fined €3,000. The judge could have given him up to five years, but concluded that there were a few loose nuts rattling around in his head. But was he bonkers? The stunts were witnessed by gazillions of people and at least a few of them may have taken his advice. Also, who can say with any certainty that the world is not going to end tomorrow?

Horan also disrupted Wimbledon and was arrested at the World Cup in Germany in 2006 before he could do one of his colourful protests. This time instead of running on to the pitch Fr Horan was reported to be planning to dance a 'peace jig' outside the stadium in Berlin before the final (in which France lost to Italy). He told Kerry's *The Kingdom* newspaper that he intended to carry posters declaring that Adolf Hitler was a good leader who was following the word of Christ, give the Hitler salute, and light a candle for Herr Hitler at the Gestapo Headquarters.

Fr Horan (who has rejected his defrocking by the

Catholic Church) first discovered the joys of Irish dancing when he was studying theology in St Peter's College in Wexford, mainly because he didn't have a great singing voice. He was ordained in 1973 by **Bishop Eamon Casey** and a year later became interested in prophesy. He left the priesthood for a short while but later returned only to be sacked for using his sermons to promote his 'sensationalist' views on the End of The World. The late 80s were to see him start his Dancing For Peace Campaign in earnest. Since then Horan has written to vast numbers of politicians and celebrities offering to dance his peace jig for them. These include soccer giant **Gary Lineker** back in 1987 and **Margaret Thatcher**, whose press secretary graciously replied telling the priest that the Iron Lady was grateful for his sterling efforts in the cause of promoting world peace.

> **During the war in Iraq the Kerryman even wrote to Saddam Hussein offering to jig up and down in front of his family and wave his legs about in the manner of a shoeless leprechaun standing on a bed of nails . . .**

During the war in Iraq the Kerryman even wrote to Saddam Hussein offering to jig up and down in front of his family and wave his legs about in the manner of a shoeless leprechaun standing on a bed of nails (that's the Scartaglin school of Irish dancing). Perhaps Saddam had an aversion to the sight of a middle-aged cleric's green underpants or maybe he had more pressing engagements to attend to, but the *seisiún* never came about.

He also offered his services to **George Bush**, a devout Christian, and **Tony Blair**. The former didn't bother replying, while Tony wrote back firmly declining the offer.

The trio may have been short-sighted in their decision not to deploy Fr Horan as the ultimate weapon in Iraq. The sight of the kilted priest lepping along in front of a column of tanks would surely have caused the enemy to die laughing.

He would have been The Perfect Weapon Of (ahem) 'Mass' Destruction.

Longest Strike In History

Ireland has endured famines and wars and still lived, albeit in a reduced state, to tell the tale and sing about it (Michael Flatley's 'Celtic Tiger' even has a stab at telling it through the medium of dance). However, a person can die of thirst quicker than hunger and, happily, our climate has never resulted in any killer droughts. One man, however, attempted to cause a localised beer drought (a draught drought) in Dun Laoghaire, which turned into the longest-running strike ever. His name was **Young** and he was fired from Downey's pub in the seaside town.

Prior to 1955, Dublin barmen had to endure pretty awful wages and working hours, so much so that it was next to impossible to rear a family and those who did suffered terrible hardships. The average salary was £7.3s for a 56-hour, six and a half-day week, with only one Sunday in four off. In July of that year the barmen instituted proceedings with their employers to negotiate for 25s extra per week, every second Sunday off and an allowance of one and a half hours for meals. The publicans responded with an offer of an increase of 8s per week and some utterances about improvements in conditions. Negotiations broke down twice and on 29 July the workers went on strike.

There had been other strikes in 1919, 1922 and 1927 that the owners had won but this time the barmen were not prepared to back down. Of the 650 public houses in Dublin, 220 were open for business on the first day of the strike. Almost 100 of these had signed agreements with the barmen and the rest were made up of non-union houses and family-run establishments. The other 430 had pickets placed on their doors and, in general, the thirsty public didn't pass these lines although they were mightily disgruntled as the hot summer progressed.

The barmen, too, were even more dismayed when they perceived that Guinness were taking the side of the publicans by not supplying extra quantities of stout to those pubs that signed deals with barmen, despite the roaring trade these houses were doing.

They organised a monster march from Parnell Square to the brewery's headquarters shouting 'strike breakers!' and other such slogans to show their displeasure. Many waved their fists and an admonishing finger or two at the petrified workers looking out of the windows.

Guinness, by now appreciating the strength of the Union, offered to mediate in the dispute and the strike was called off after five weeks with the barmen getting the extra money and more time off, proving that they did, indeed, have 'homes to go to'.

This, however, was not The Longest Bar Strike Ever. That took place outside of Downey's pub on Upper George's Street, Dun Laoghaire and lasted over fourteen years. The dispute happened when **Old Mr Downey** gave one of his barmen, Young Mr Young, the boot in February 1939 without any apparent good reason. He subsequently refused the union's demand to reinstate his employee and a strike was called on 6 March. Despite the union prohibiting its members from working on the premises, 400 applied when Old Man Downey advertised for four new hands. The stubborn publican's business suffered not a jot despite the presence of picketers outside his door. In fact it may have increased as the dispute wore on and sightseers dropped in for a pint and a look at the strikers. As the years wore on, the story of Downey's pub gained international renown and tourists flocked to it, making Old Man Downey even more resolute in his determination not to negotiate. For fourteen years the picketers walked up and down in front of the pub, eating sandwiches made by the locals. Some say the pub even supplied a few to encourage the strikers to keep their strength up and carry on protesting.

Before Mr Downey pulled his last pint in June 1953 he was quoted as saying that for all he cared the picketers could stay outside the pub until the day he died. They could even march at his funeral, he declared. They did both.

The new owner and the union quickly reached an

agreement and the end of Ireland's and the world's longest strike was celebrated in the bar on 27 November, 1953 as the last of the picketers went through his final paces outside.

This fine old shrine to Dublin pub life and the working man's struggle to improve his lot was replaced by a shopping centre in the mid-1970s.

INTERESTING FACTS

- Stillorgan Shopping Centre was the first to be built in the state and opened for business in 1966.
- Guinness' St James's Gate Brewery occupies the site where, in medieval times, pious Dubs held an annual boozing session every 25 July to celebrate St. James' feastday.
- No other brewery in the world uses as much roasted barley as Guinness. It even prepares its own.
- The 'Guinness is Good for You' slogan was born in the 1920s when the company did some market research to find out what people liked about the black brew. The overwhelming answer was that people 'felt good' when they had their pint. While it certainly has a relaxing effect on stressed nerves, large quantities of the bottle-conditioned variety have been known to have an unpleasant laxative effect due to the live yeast content – the squitters, or 'flock of bats effect', in other words.

Shortest Time To Drink A Pint Of Guinness

The ending of the 1955 pub strike may have resulted in some speedy drinking by thirsty patrons as they got back into the swing of things, but none can match the speed-drinking prowess of a gentleman by the name of **Patrick Carelli**. He is credited with drinking a pint of black stout in an incredible 2.94 seconds at Keeling's Pub in Donabate, County Dublin, on 31 March 2001. Not only that, he also managed to set the record for the . . . Shortest Time To Drink Two Pints of Guinness.

Shortest Time To Drink Two Pints of Guinness

An amazing 6.9 seconds at the same venue on the same date. Mr Carelli may also have set the time for fastest regurgitation of two pints of Guinness. If not, he's some man.

Shortest-Lived Newspaper

Newspapers have been an integral part of Irish life for the past three centuries since the publication of the very first periodical newssheet entitled *An Account of the Chief Occurrences of Ireland*, in February 1660, by Sir Charles Coote. It wasn't a terribly good newspaper and folded (as all paper objects do) the following month. In 1685 *The Newsletter* began publishing in Dublin and managed to stay open for seven months. Then in 1699, Cornelius

Carter got the modern era of newspaper publishing off to a flying start with his Flying Post which ran for twenty-five years ushering in the age of Faulkner's Dublin Journal (1725–1825) and Saunders's *News-Letter* (1755-1879).

Paper publishing suffered a serious economic setback during the Napoleonic era and the 1798 Rebellion, but by the 1850s, circulations began to rise again. This was largely due to advances in paper manufacturing and print technology (which helped reduce production costs), and the lifting of taxes on adverts (which brought in more revenue for the publisher). The decline of the Irish tongue and the spread of literacy as more people opted to learn English following The Education Acts also increased the readerships.

In 1859 Major Lawrence Knox launched the country's first penny newspaper, *The Irish Times*. Forty-six years later, the *Irish Independent* started publishing and in 1931 the *Irish Press* was set up by Eamon de Valera, closing in 1995.

Ireland (at time of publication) has nine morning daily newspapers, five of which are published in Dublin: the *Irish Independent, The Irish Times, The Star, The Sun* and *The Irish Daily Mail*. Three are published north of the border: *The News Letter, The Irish News* and the *Daily Mirror*. One, *The Examiner*, is published in Cork while there are two morning Metro Papers in Dublin: *Herald AM* and *Metro*. There are three evening newspapers across the country: the *Evening Herald* (Dublin), The *Belfast Telegraph*, and *The Evening Echo* (Cork).

There are also seven leading Sunday newspapers produced in Dublin: *The Sunday Independent*, *The Sunday World*, *The Sunday Tribune*, *The Sunday Business Post*, *The Irish Mail on Sunday* and the *Irish Daily Star Sunday*. *The Sunday Life* is published in Belfast.

As stated above, this is the case at time of publication. The Irish newspaper reading public has a funny way of encouraging papers to spring up almost overnight and vanish as quickly. Take for example, *Daily Ireland*, which started printing in January 2005 to cover news stories from an 'Irish republican' viewpoint. Although short-lived, it gave it a good go and ceased publication after bringing out its 475th edition on 7 September 2006.

During its run, *Daily Ireland* managed to raise a few hackles with its exceptionally pro-Sinn Féin stance, which led to the Republic's then Minister for Justice, Michael McDowell claiming that it was supported by the IRA and comparing it, on the Government website, to the Nazi party newspaper *Völkischer Beobachter*. 'Will it be to Irish democracy what the *Völkischer Beobachter* was to pre-WWII German democracy?' he asked.

This in turn led to a threat of legal action for libel by the publishers of the paper, who also maintained that his comments put the staff in danger from loyalist groups.

No other paper in the history of the state can claim to have made such a large impact over such a short period of time – not even the colourful 64-page *Dublin Daily* over its meagre 90-edition run from March to July 2003. Although it has the distinction of being the only dedicated Dublin paper ever to switch from being a daily (with over 70,000 copies available from as early as 1 am) to an evening paper with a different name (*Dublin Evening*) in the space of three months.

Nor for that matter could the *Xpress* (May to September 1995), set up by laid-off journalists from the *Irish Press* or *The Leader* (November 1995 to April 1996) which became the *Evening News* (May to September 1996) which also had *Irish Press* ties. The *Dublin Tribune* managed to limp on from 1989 to 1992, but the most shortlived paper of them all was the *Daily News*.

Launched by *Sunday Tribune* owner and magazine mogul, Hugh McLaughlin to a loud fanfare in 1982, the *Daily News* proved a mess and a financial disaster from the start, despite having attracted a number of hardened hacks onto its staff. It gobbled up resources at such a rate that it actually forced the fledgling *Tribune* into liquidation. The latter, at this point, had been building on its own readership.

Poorly designed, printed and thought out, it was put to bed permanently after a minor storm that followed the printing of a picture of disgraced car manufacturer, John De Lorean's topless wife on the front page. Mrs De Lorean could have been topless, bottomless, armless or legless for all anyone could make out due to the print quality of the paper, but the snap annoyed and offended more readers than the paper could afford. In a matter of days (and after only nine editions) it was relegated to the fish and chip shops of history.

Longest Lived Newspaper

The *Belfast Newsletter* first hit the streets in 1737 and is one of the oldest continuously published newspapers in the world.

Longest Name

Sean D Dublin Bay Rockall Loftus. The former councillor, Lord Mayor of Dublin, Independent TD and lecturer changed his name by deed poll to highlight opposition over plans to build an oil refinery in Dublin Bay and to assert Ireland's ownership of the disputed, mineral-rich Rockall Island. He also added 'Christian Democrat' at one stage and prompted debates in the Seanad over whether his name was too long for the register. His presence at public meetings, while welcomed by all concerned with the capital's environmental issues, has always been dreaded by the person responsible for making the name tags.

Shortest Book

This one, if we had our way.

Shortest Shorts

Those worn by GAA players. Occasionally you can see someone's mickey worming its way out of the sides of them. They also wear the shortest socks, probably to prove they are too manly to wear shinpads.

Shortest Entry In This Book

This one.

Greatest

Greatest Comeback Since JC

No contest. In terms of comebacks, Charles James Haughey, the most intriguing Irish politician of the twentieth century, makes Lazarus look like he'd just woken up from a snooze when Jesus called around.

Haughey's career appeared over before it began in earnest as a result of the Arms Crisis and subsequent trial on 28 May 1970. His demise began with the start of the Troubles when, in answer to the growing disturbances in the North, Jack Lynch's government established a cabinet subcommittee to organise emergency assistance for the Catholics in that part of the island. Haughey, then Minister for Finance, and Neil 'Blunderbuss' Blaney, were members of the subcommittee, but disagreed with Lynch's apparently cautious approach to the problem. They were accused of using the allocated funds instead to import IR£100,000 (€127,000) worth of weapons for the Provos. The shipment was called off at the last minute when it was realised that they couldn't be slipped past customs officials at Dublin Airport.

Lynch subsequently gave Haughey and Blaney the boot. The Minister for Social Welfare, Kevin Boland – whose father Harry was a ringer for American actor Aidan Quinn – resigned in protest. The Minister for Justice, Micheál Ó Móráin, was also asked to resign and claimed later that, despite reports to the contrary, he had informed Lynch of the individuals involved in the plan.

CJ and Blaney went on trial along with army intelligence officer Captain James Kelly, Belgian businessman Albert Luykx and Northern Republican John Kelly. By 23 October 1970 all four had been cleared. However, since Defence Minister, Jim Gibbons, had been in direct conflict with Haughey during the trial regarding the sanctioning of the arms, the latter's acquittal left a cloud hanging over his name.

The resignations and sackings left four vacancies in cabinet, and left Haughey languishing on the back benches. Boland and Blaney were both thrown out of Fianna Fáil in 1970 and 1971 respectively. Embittered and determined not to simply fade away, Blaney went on to found Independent Fianna Fáil and was a constant buzzing in the ears of his former party until his death in 1995.

Haughey, on the other hand, managed not only to stay in the party and ride out the storm with Lynch but, Faust-like, returned to ministerial office, and eventually succeeded Lynch as fourth party leader in 1979.

After waiting in the long grass for five years, CJ finally got recalled to the front benches as Spokesman on Health and Social Welfare in 1975 – much to the dismay of the general public. It was enough of a springboard to relaunch his career and when Fianna Fáil returned to power with a massive majority in 1977, Haughey was made Minister for Health & Social Welfare. In was in this post that he famously referred to his *Family Planning Bill*, which allowed married people to buy Rubber Johnnies with a doctor's prescription, as 'an Irish solution to an Irish problem'.

> **Swashbuckling, conniving, corrupt and charming in equal measure (legend has it he once patted Margaret Thatcher's bottom), CJ served three terms in office . . .**

The next step was to get rid of Lynch, which he did with the help of the **Gang of Five** – Tom McEllistrim Jr, Seán Doherty, Jackie Fahey, Mark Killilea and pet food king, Albert Reynolds. In December 1979 Lynch announced his resignation and Haughey beat off the popular George Colley by 44 votes to 38 to become the sixth Taoiseach of the Republic.

Swashbuckling, conniving, corrupt and charming in equal measure (legend has it he once patted Margaret Thatcher's bottom), CJ served three terms in office: 1979 to 1981, March 1982 to December 1982, and 1987 to 1992. Throughout those years he operated like a modern-day Irish Chieftain who had been dipped in

3-in-1 oil and then coated in Teflon, such was his talent for wriggling out of a tight hole. The coating finally wore off in 1992 when the Minister for Justice, Sean Doherty, went on the RTÉ show *Nighthawks* and told the nation that Haughey had authorised the tapping of political journalists' phones in the early 1980s – a scandal CJ had successfully denied back in 1983. The PDs threatened to pull out of Government and CJ eventually resigned. His passing was to mark the end of the 'Great Gombeenism' era of Irish politics, when a nod and a wink would get you your heart's desire and the nation wouldn't be any the wiser.

Even his detractors admit that he left an impressive political legacy. The Castlebar-man, whose own family fled Derry after a sectarian attack on their farm, is credited with starting the current Peace Process. He is also cited as the man who paved the way for the **Celtic Tiger**. However, after telling everyone in the 1980s to tighten their belts for the tough times ahead, it was subsequently disclosed in the late 1990s that he had been loosening his own belt to allow for all the cream he was skimming off the top.

What's surprising about this is the fact that nobody noticed that Haughey was living life as a millionaire on a politician's salary, with a rambling eighteenth-century house in County Dublin, as well as a yacht, a private island off the southwest of Ireland and several racehorses. At the Moriarty Tribunal it was revealed that he had received more than IR£8m (€10m) over an 18-year period from various benefactors including supermarket king, Ben Dunne. Amazingly, none of the payments was ever linked to favours. It appears that the millionaires just gave him what he wanted as 'tributes' to a man whose policies helped them flourish.

After decades of fine dining and riding his horse around his stately Kinsealy pile, CJ made his second great escape on 13 June 2006. The Charvet shirt-loving *bête noir* of Irish politics passed away without ever going on trial for his dodgy financial affairs.

However, there was much speculation immediately after his death as to whether he really had 'left the building' Elvis-style. According to an article in the *Evening Herald*, it was 'brown trousers time' in Leinster House as staff reported a number of spooky happenings that coincided with the exact time of CJ popping his clogs. Automatic doors into the Taoiseach's department stopped working and a segment of ceiling collapsed inside the building as Bertie Ahern was informing TDs about CJ's passing. And it wasn't just a little crumb of plaster that fell. In true Haughey style, a massive wooden beam went crashing to the floor just as people were passing underneath it.

Word on the Ouija board is that he's already planning his next comeback.

INTERESTING FACTS

- Charlie once described Editorials in *The Irish Times* as being written by 'an old lady sitting in the bath, with the water getting colder and colder around her fanny'.
- If you reverse the initials 'CJ' you get those of a man who made THE most famous comeback in history. Coincidental?

Greatest Feat Of Memory

On an island renowned for most of its inhabitants' predilection to battering their brain cells to smithereens with alcohol, there is a surprising number of Irish people with exceptional memories. RTE sports commentating legend **Jimmy Magee** is one of them. Known as the Memory Man, Jimmy can rattle off amazing facts about football matches, camogie clashes, boxing bouts, teams, scores and old stories with incredible ease. Sounds like a great man to get stuck with at a party, doesn't he? Jimmy, however, doesn't drink, which may account for the clarity of his brain.

A man renowned for his fondness for a drop of the 'crathur', on the other hand, was the late **Brian Lenihan** TD, popular rogue and friend of CJ Haughey's. Thanks to Brian, we now have the phrase 'on mature recollection' as part of our political lexicon. On 31 October 1990, as Tánaiste and presidential candidate, he repeatedly used it in a live interview on RTÉ's *Six One News*.

If Lenihan was a super-charged political engine, then his memory was like a manic windscreen wiper, to-ing and fro-ing between two versions of any event that could have brought down the government of Garret FitzGerald in the early 1980s. Lenihan was a close friend of **President Paddy Hillery** and in January 1982 the 'real Boss', CJ Haughey, requested him to phone the Áras to pressurise his chum into refusing FitzGerald a parliamentary dissolution.

Haughey was desperate for the Dáil to fall because of a challenge to his leadership by **Charlie 'Mad Magazine' McCreevy**. Had Hillery gone the dissolution route – which he didn't – Garret the Good would have had to resign, allowing CJ to form a government and step into the role of Taoiseach. Much to Lenihan's discredit, he did as he was bid and made the calls – which he later freely admitted when questioned about it.

Then the 1990 presidential campaign came around and Brian's memory began to falter. In the heat of his campaign against Mary Robinson his story changed and in October he told the *Irish Press* and RTÉ's *Questions and Answers* that he had played 'no hand, act or part' in the attempted pressuring of Paddy Hillery. Everything he had said about the affair prior to this, he claimed, had been 'off the record' to hacks and therefore non-attributable. There was one hitch however. Back in May of the same year, Lenihan had confirmed his participation to post-graduate student journalist Jim Duffy, who was doing a series of articles on the Irish Presidency for *The Irish Times*. Which version of events was the truth?

The storm broke and on prime time news an ill-looking Lenihan stared out of magic telly land and told the people of Ireland repeatedly that 'on mature recollection' his most recent version of events, and not the earlier one (to Jim Duffy), was correct. That is, after eight years of telling people that he had phoned the Áras, he had suddenly remembered that he hadn't done anything of the sort. How silly of him.

The phrase is now generally used as a soft way of saying: 'Bugger it, I'm a liar. You know I'm a liar, but let me off the hook this time, will you?'

Whereas most Irish people were rather fond of Lenihan and would have liked to cut him some slack, his lack of trustworthiness lost him the election, and his good friend CJ cut him loose.

So much for friends in politics. But then Lenihan – a bit of chancer himself – knew the measure of CJ better than most. He was the kind of man to give you the shirt off his back . . . and then ask you to pay for it.

In typically duplicitous fashion, when Lenihan was desperately in need of a liver transplant, Haughey went around his business cronies with a begging bowl to raise funds . . . and then skimmed some of the moolah off the top to pay a bill for his beloved Charvet shirts.

It's unlikely Brian ever forgot that little matter.

Greatest Weak Minds Thinking Alike

Occasionally when you're working on the production side of a busy newspaper (designing pages, translating reporters' copy etc), you get a story that writes its own headline immediately. You all look at each other on the back bench and scramble to be the first to say it aloud. For example when this hack worked in the sports department of the *Irish Press* he was lucky enough to get the match report for the St Patrick's Athletic v Shamrock Rovers match (1–0) on the Paddy's Bank Holiday weekend – 'Shamrock wilts on St Pat's Day'. On another occasion a story about *The Late Late Show* host Pat Kenny talking about his fitness regime and battle with the bulge presented itself – 'It's the Weight, Weight Show' and so on.

Sometimes two of the red-top tabloids (*Sun*, *Mirror*, *Star*) will have similar headlines on Page One as they tend to chase the same style of lead stories having the same target readership. Never would you get all three tabloids with exactly the same lead headline on the same day. Until 3 February, 2006.

'GREAT BALLS OF FIRE'

whooped *The Sun*, with *The Star* and *Mirror* echoing its cry.

'Footie hot-shot wins €9K after pitch lime burns up his privates'

A TOP politician won €9,000 compo yesterday after burning his dangly bits in a SOCCER MATCH . . .

Thus ran the subhead and introduction to an event (that happened in 1993 by the way) concerning amateur player and Donegal County Council Chairman, Dessie Larkin. Poor Dessie got the distinct impression that his testicles were on fire as he came off the pitch after playing with Bonagee Celtic in the FAI Junior Cup. His privates had, in fact, been spattered with the lime used to mark out the boundaries of the field of play. As there were no showers at Drumbar FC in Rockfield, Donegal Town, Dessie drove home in considerable pain with the lime still on his scrotum. When he got home he applied some Sudocream to the area, took painkillers and went straight to bed.

The court in Letterkenny heard that the next morning poor Dessie awoke with his shorts stuck to him but bravely went to work anyway. There, the plant nurse packed him off to see a doctor who gave him antibiotics and morphine and, in turn, packed him off to hospital.

Dessie had suffered a lime burn, which can be a very nasty thing. Especially on one's nuts.

Referee Tony Gillroy told the court that there had been no instructions for mixing the offending lime with water. On top of this, because of inclement weather the pitch had been marked not once but twice, two hours before the start of the match. Normally it would have been done the day before. As the lining machine was broken, the solution had to be brushed on to the grass, further aggravating things. The judge sympathised with the Independent Fianna Fáil councillor and found against the Football Association of Ireland.

Dessie said he still gets uncomfortable around his

privates while walking.

If your eyes have stopped watering and you're able to read on, it might interest you to know that the version of this story in the *Sun* was also responsible for a classic case of 'juxtaposition'. (This is where two unrelated stories or pictures appear side-by-side and seem to be referring to each other – for example a picture of English model Jordan sticking her boobs out alongside a story about Food Aid for Africa or a piece on the extinction of the Blue Tit.) In the case of *The Sun*, the 'Great Balls of Fire' story continued from Page One onto Page 8, with the abbreviated heading 'Footie Fireballs', juxtapositioned beside pictures of two actors dancing in the RTÉ drama *Stardust*, recalling the tragic nightclub inferno that claimed the lives of 48 teenagers in 1981.

From 'Great Balls of Fire' to 'Great Balls Up'.

Greatest Revolutionary Poet To Be Thrown Off The 7A Bus

Christopher Daybell, who was thrown off the bus near Monkstown, County Dublin. If you haven't heard of him then there's no point explaining.

Most and Least

Most Successful Bog Snorkeller

Everybody, if Christy Moore is to be believed, needs a break. Climb a mountain, he says, or jump in a lake, or thrash about in a dirty, foul-smelling, leech-infested, water-filled ditch in Wales – on a bike.

OK, he never suggested the latter, but this is exactly how some Irish people like to let their hair down. The pastime is called Mountain Bike Bog Snorkelling and one Irishwoman in particular so enjoys this 'sport' that she is a World Champion at it.

In July 2004 biology teacher **Julia Galvin** won the Ladies' World Championship in Llanwrtyd Wells, Wales when she cycled 40 m through 2 m-deep water in a large boghole in a mere 2 min 36 sec. She and the bike were weighed down by lead, and a snorkel was attached to her hat. It will come as no surprise to learn that Julia is from Kerry.

That handicap aside, the bouncy lady from Listowel took up swimming in her 20s as a cure for painful injuries she received in two car accidents. She has since become a regular Irish representative in Orthodox Bog Snorkelling – which, frankly, is just for wimps compared to Mountain Bike Bog Snorkelling. In the Orthodox Bog Snorkelling World Championships competitors have only to swim two lengths of the 54-m Waen Rhydd bog without using conventional swimming strokes. They are not even required to carry puncture repair kits.

The competition celebrated its 20th anniversary in 2005 and had a record 150 entrants, which is an impressive amount of people all on the bog at the same time. Heaven forbid that Julia was just a one-trick pony when it came to the exotic world of eccentric sports. A week before she defended her title, the 30-something-year-old along with **Paul Roberts**, the Irish Strongman Champion, represented Ireland in the World Wife-Carrying Championships in Sonkajarvi, Finland. The event is a 250 m hurdle over grass, sand, asphalt and water. The competition, based on the nineteenth-century practice of villagers stealing women from neighbouring towns, has strict entry requirements. The minimum weight for the wife is 49 kg, and if the woman is lighter the man gets a heavy rucksack clapped to his back. If a contestant drops his wife the couple gains a 15 sec time fault, and not having fun leads to instant disqualification. (Those crrrazy Finns)

Sadly, Julia and Paul, who weighed in at a combined and cuddly 120 kg didn't win, but they delighted the

8,000 spectators with their brave effort in a time of 4 minutes 22 sec.

Julia took it all in her stride and indicated her intention to train for the World Arse Sledding Championship in Neudorf, Germany. The event involves sledding down an icy mountain in lederhosen. Reportedly Julia got an engineer to design special lederhosen with thin leather ski blades on the rear.

Groovy, Julia.

INTERESTING FACTS

- Kerry is the second largest exporter of industrial muck in the EU.
- Wales is famous for coal mines and Ireland is famous for bogs. There are no plans to introduce a World Coal Mine Diving Championship in Kerry, despite the rumours.

Most Dublin Of Dubliners

They say you're not a real Dubliner if you weren't born between the North and South Circular Roads, or raised hard and fast in Pimlico in the Rebel Liberties, or some other such claptrap. If that is the case and the area you inhabit defines who you are, then the truest of true blue Dubs have to be ... the penguins in Dublin Zoo – or the Yazoo, as it is commonly called.

According to the Irish Tourism Board[12], 'Dublin was

[12] http://www.discoverireland.com/gb/ireland-places-to-go/areas-and-cities/dublin-city/overview/ (accessed on 3 July 2006)

originally called *Dubh Linn* meaning Black Pool. The original pool is the oldest known in Northern Europe and now forms the centerpiece of the penguin enclosure in Dublin Zoo.' So there you have it, the penguins are true blue, black–and–white Dubs.

The problem with the previous statement, however, is that it's a pile of penguin poo.

And so, to our history books. Dublin is a schizophrenic little city with two monickers: *Baile Átha Cliath* and *Dubh Linn/Dyflinn/*Dublin. The former, meaning the Ford of the Hurdles, was a river crossing on the south bank at the site of present day Church Street/Fr. Matthew Bridge. The ford was made of wattles woven together and anchored by posts to the Liffey bed, and hence gave its name to the nearby fishing and farming settlement.

The river was at least four times wider than it is now and was known as *An Ruirthech*, meaning The Stormy One. It certainly lived up to its name in 770AD, when a raiding party of Ulstermen was drowned as it returned victorious from a battle with the Dubs.

At another site 1 km East, which in the Iron Age would have covered O'Connell Street and Trinity College, another settlement flourished at the estuary where it entered the bay. The area was named after a Black Pool on the Poddle that fed into the river on Dame Street and provided a sheltered harbour for trading out of Dublin Bay.

If you're serious about finding the true source of Dublin's name then you need go no further than the tweezered lawn of Dublin Castle's Dubh Linn Garden which now occupies the site. Unlike Wood Quay, which was destroyed by the horrendous Civic Offices in the 1970s, this hugely important Viking site has never been built on.

And therein lies the problem – Dame Street is 3.2 km from the Zoo, where the Irish Tourist Board tells us the original 'pool' can be found under the guardianship of the penguins. Dublin Zoo is also on the opposite side of the river. And so we must forgive the Zoo's penguins for believing they dwell in *Dubh Linn*. If the Tourist Board can't get it right, how could the penguins be expected to? Much to their credit, the penguins have resisted the traditions practiced in other well-known Black Pools and do not wear kiss-me-quick hats or knotted handkerchiefs on their heads.

Much to their credit, the penguins have resisted the traditions practised in other well-known Black Pools and do not wear kiss-me-quick hats or knotted handkerchiefs on their heads.

For this small mercy alone, *Erindipity* has no intention of disabusing the poor creatures of the notion that they are The Most Dublin of Dubliners.

Besides, the Zoo has another, equally compelling, claim to fame . . . the most famous Dubliner of all time lived and worked there for two years.

Most Lionised Lion

Cairbre the Lion was born in Dublin Zoo on 20 March 1927. After entertaining the good citizens of the Fair City for two years he was carted off to the MGM studios in Hollywood, USA, had voice coaching and became an A-List star, roaring his head off at the start of hundreds of movies.

Unfortunately, fame went to Cairbre's head and on arrival in Tinseltown he promptly forgot his roots and changed his name to Leo. After a string of scandalous affairs, a second Dublin Zoo lion was selected and filmed to replace Cairbre, but no one knows if that footage was ever used as they both looked identical.

Despite a remarkable similarity to Luke Kelly, Cairbre/Leo didn't really look very 'Dublin'. On the other hand, Penguins – when they're lying on their backs – look like spilt pints of Guinness. And what could be more Dublin than that?

INTERESTING FACTS

- Lions don't generally eat penguins. This is because lions live in Africa and penguins live in Antarctica.
- In the summer of 1986 a group of youths threw a Penguin into the lions' den at Dublin Zoo. It wasn't eaten, however, as the lions couldn't get the wrapper off.

Most Irish Of Animals

Many wild animals found in Ireland are descended from the first influx of creatures after the last Ice Age 9,000 years ago, before 'Proto-Paddy' loped into view. Others have been introduced intentionally or otherwise by man. The rabbit (*coinín*) was brought here by the Normans 750 years ago and bred for food. Realising what fate awaited them, they took the opportunity to get some last minute action and humped each other like mad. This resulted in an explosion in their population and soon they had shagged off to every nook and cranny on the island. Can't blame them, can you?

The fallow deer (*fia bán*) was also introduced by the Normans, who liked their hunting (hunting cows, apparently, was too easy), and the black rat (*francach dubh*) – cause of the fourteenth-century Black Death plague. So too was the house mouse (*luch thí*), which conveniently rhymes with itself. The grey squirrel (*lora glas*) is new too and was brought to County Longford in the twentieth century. The red squirrel (*lora dearg*) on the other hand is native to Ireland, although it had to be reintroduced in the nineteenth century when it became extinct due to hunting and deforestation. The bank vole is also a newcomer and only arrived, probably by boat, in the 1950s (so we're not giving it an Irish name, the little thug).

Our other native animals are: Irish stoat (*easóg Éireannach*), natterjack toad (*cnádán*), pygmy shrew (*dallóg fraoigh*), pine martin (*cat crainn*), common and grey seals (*rón beag agus glas*), hedgehog (*gráinneog*), field mouse (*luch fhéir*), common newt (*earc sléibhe*), porpoise (*muc mhara*), badger (*broc*), otter (*dobhrán*), red fox (*sionnach*), red deer (*fia rua*), feral goats (*fia ghabhar*) (the feral goats on Dalkey Island are called Noigel and Penelope, roight?), viviparous lizard (*earc luachra*), Connemara pony (*capailín Chonamara*), Daubenton's, natterer, pipistrelle, Leisler, lesser horseshoe and whiskered bat (*ialtóg*), dolphin (*deilf*) and killer whale (*cráin dubh*).

There are other, less well-known, creatures native to Ireland. They are the Connemara horse-eel ('stay away from the shore, Nora, or the horse-eel will get you!!! Good God it's too late.' Moral: Never try to outrun a Connemara horse-eel), the Kerry mountain worm (part dragon, it lives by pools) and the Shannon peiste (drags fisherman to their deaths). Unfortunately, no one has managed to capture or photograph any of the above.

The most Irish of Irish animals is our hare (*giorria Éireannach*), which is a type of Arctic hare as distinct from the brown hare of Britain. As such, it arrived with the first fauna after the Ice Age and so is 9,000 or so years old. It's a sporty little thing and can run at speeds of up to 60 km an hour. Every winter it gets involved in boxing bouts with its fellow hares as part of the mating process – with the females, we hasten to add. That is, they mate with the females and box each other – but not at the same time.

Anyway, as it likes a fight, is into racing and has appeared on an Irish coin (the threepenny bit), the Irish Hare is the Most Irish of Animals.

Least Irish Of Animals

These are the main contenders: the mink, the kangaroo, various snakes, big cats and that horrible creature, the mosquito.

Let's start with the **mink**. This unpleasant little bugger is a native of the North American continent but has become an unwelcome inhabitant of the Irish countryside. This is largely due to its release into the wild by Mink Farm protestors. Due to their incredible aggression (the minks, that is, not the protestors) they have thrived in our temperate climate. Mink breed once a year with an average litter of six kits. They live anywhere from rabbit burrows (after they've slaughtered the poor bunnies) to old sheds or even moored boats.

> . . . many believe that: 'the Mink should DIE! DIE, I TELLS YOU!!!' In fact, such is the eagerness to wipe out these potential fashion items that hunters are not even offered a bounty on them.

They mainly dine on fish and birds but are quite partial to killing just for the fun of it. Poultry farmers frequently awake in the morning to find entire chicken coops wiped out by this diminutive menace. It is for this reason, and because it is only a blow-in that many believe that: 'the Mink should DIE! DIE, I TELLS YOU!!!' In fact, such is the eagerness to wipe out these potential fashion items that hunters are not even offered a bounty on them.

The **kangaroo**, on the other hand, is a very welcome visitor although it tends not to last long in the wild. In

2006 Irish kangaroo spotters did a treble take after three Skippys hopped it while their minders' backs were turned. The first legged it from an Aussie Circus in County Cork after its pen door was left open. **Sydney** (for that was his name) spent six days on the run enjoying the sights of glamorous Belgooly before he was caught after a not very dignified half-hour chase across the fields. He was given a warm welcome on his return to the circus with everyone lining up to hug him, only to discover the reason why he hadn't managed to outrun his captors – sixteen cans of Blunden Village Super Strong Extra Ballrot Cider secreted in his pouch. Disgraced, he was given a stern talking to and sent to bed with an ice pack.

Two other kangaroos had a near escape after running free on the Northside of Dublin, something most sane people wouldn't dream of doing. Stunned Northsiders thought their own cans of Blunden Village Extra Strong had been spiked when a kangaroo bounced past them in Portmarnock and hopped onto a nearby green in a suburban estate. It transpired that Joey and his companion had done a runner shortly after their owner had moved into the area. They were both eventually tied down (not literally of course, it's just a Rolf Harris reference) and lived happily ever after. Or as happily as they could after developing a 'Howya' accent and a Smack problem from their time spent on the run[13].

Thankfully Smacked-out kangaroos don't bite, unlike the highly poisonous **horn-nosed viper** from Greece. One of these lethal 25 cm charmers was found in a box

[13] To the people of North Dublin: stop complaining, we've been slagging off country folk throughout this book. Just redressing the balance.

of tiles imported from Greece to Cork by workers at a building site in Ballyduff. The *Irish Independent* reported that the reptile, whose venom can kill within two hours, was curled up in the box and caused a little 'brown overalls' time for the shocked tilers.

The sneaky snake was kept under wraps in a secret location and was apparently quietly moved to Dublin Zoo, said a 'source', who was wearing a natty new pair of snakeskin shoes.

Another avid 'biter' is the **mosquito**, which appears to be better at surviving here in the 'Wild' than 'roos and snakes. The 'Wild' in this case being Drogheda – Ireland's mossie capital.

Due to a plant-loving lord, climate change and cheap package holidays, more and more mosquitos are adapting to conditions here after being inadvertently brought home in suitcases from the Costa del Sol etc. Most cases of mossie bites have so far been confined to the areas north of Dublin, and, in particular, Drogheda.

The *Drogheda Independent* of 14 July 2006 reported that mosquitos were causing havoc in the town, with young and old suffering bites and, in some cases, requiring medical attention. One local councillor reported being bitten all over his body and around the eye, which subsequently swelled up and necessitated a trip to the doctor in the middle of the night. Another woman even ended up on a drip after her bites became infected. The Dublin Road area was the worst hit with residents buying huge amounts of anti-histamine creams and tablets from the local chemists.

There are now twenty species of mosquito living in Ireland and, apart from global warming and holidaymakers one of the chief culprits for bringing them to our shores was the former owner of Malahide Castle, **Lord Talbot**, who imported some plants for his gardens and, unfortunately, inherited some mossies into the bargain. This particular breed of mosquito currently likes nothing better than snacking on the inhabitants of the Malahide / Portmarnock / Swords estuary area.

Damp conditions in Drogheda are also favourable for the flourishing of the little suckers.

Another reason for mosquitos liking Drogheda and Dublin's Northside could be a widespread Vitamin B deficiency in these places. (Too many kebabs in the diet and not enough multi-vitamins.) Mossies hate the smell of Vitamin B (really) and turn their noses up at it.

For some weird reason they don't mind the smell of a Northsider. How perplexing.

INTERESTING FACT

- The allergic reaction suffered by some of us bitten by mossies is not caused by the bite itself but by the anti-clotting agent the mosquito uses so that we don't feel ourselves being bitten.

Least Mexican Of Mexican Bandits

El Zorro – or The Fox – was the masked alter ego of Don Diego de la Vega, a slick nobleman who was a wiz with a sword, liked wearing black, and beating up stupid, fat soldiers and carving a 'Z' in their pants. He lived in California, at a time when it was ruled by Spain, and fought the authorities on behalf of the poor and oppressed. Think Robin Hood with a good dental hygienist, a tan and a whip. His catchphrase was 'A-ha!!' or something like that.

That's the official Zorro, who was dreamed up by writer **Johnston McCulley** and first flashed his weapon across the pages of *All Story Magazine* in 'The Curse of Capistrano' in 1919, inspiring the classic TV series starring Guy Mitchell and movies like *The Mask of Zorro* (1998) with Antonio Banderas and Anthony Hopkins.

The real Zorro was an entirely different proposition. In fact he was a red-bearded Paddy from Wexford. **William Lamport**, the child prodigy of a wealthy seventeenth-century Catholic landowner, was sent to London to be secretly tutored by the Jesuits during the Penal Law years.

At the age of thirteen Lamport was arrested for publishing seditious Catholic pamphlets but managed to escape aboard a ship bound for France. En route he was captured by pirates and spent the next two years splicing the main brace before jumping ship and resuming his education at an Irish school in Santiago de Compostela in Spain. As gifted as he was daring, our twinkly-eyed Irish Zorro learned to speak fourteen languages by the age of 21, unlike the screen Zorro who only spoke English with a Spanish accent.

Lamport endeared himself to the Spanish King Philip IV when he 'persuaded' 250 pirates in two ships to swear their allegiance to his crown and then distinguished himself, renamed 'Guillen Lombardo', during the Thirty Years War at the Battle of Nordlingen in 1634.

Lamport is believed to have been a bit of a man for the ladies and caused a scandal when he was caught having an affair with a noblewoman. He was packed off to Mexico to work as a spy and it was there that his life turned another corner and he came into conflict with his Spanish masters. Coming from a country oppressed by a foreign colonial power he began to sympathise and work on behalf of the Indians and black slaves who came to call him Zorro for his knack of evading capture.

In 1642 as he was about to announce his engagement to another noblewoman, the Inquisition (boo, hiss etc and so forth) accused him of plotting to overthrow the Spanish authorities, free the slaves and set himself up as king. He was sentenced to ten years in jail but escaped after eight years. Unable to fight his rebellious streak Zorro was recaptured two days later when he stole out to stick anti-Inquisition posters on the walls of Mexico City. In 1659 the Inquisition condemned him as a heretic and ordered him to be burned at the stake.

Our wily Irish Zorro, not prepared to let himself be humiliated in such a fashion, struggled out of his bonds, and strangled himself to death with his iron collar. Neither method, it should be noted, is a particularly pleasant way to go.

Lamport was only 44 years old but had lived an even more adventurous life than his fictional namesake and will be remembered as the author of the first 'Declaration of Independence' in the Americas. This charter promised the Mexicans racial equality, land reform and a democratically elected leader nearly a century before the one signed by George Washington and his contemporaries.

There have been numerous attempts to bring the Irish Zorro's life story to the big screen, but nobody could persuade Antonio Banderas to star in a movie called *The Little Bobbly Woollen Aran Hat of Zorro*.

Mickey Rourke did, apparently, consider taking the lead role in *The Balaclava of Zorro* in which our hero returns to Ireland and slashes the words 'Brits Out' on the pants of bumbling, fat British Soldiers.

Most Burgled House

In 1978 **Sir Alfred and Lady Beit** decided to throw open the doors and hand over Russborough House, Blessington, County Wicklow and its €40m art collection to the Irish people, a move that some took a little too literally. The priceless collection has been targeted by thieves on four occasions, once by infamous criminal **Martin 'The General' Cahill**.

Sir Alfred had inherited the 150 paintings and other works of art from Otto Beit who was the co-founder of the De Beers diamond-mining company. In 1952 he bought the magnificent 1741 Palladian mansion to house his beloved collection. There must have been many times when he wished he hadn't.

The house was first burgled on 26 April 1974 by British heiress **Dr Rose Dugdale** and four accomplices. They struck late in the evening, holding up the Beits at gunpoint and taking nineteen paintings worth IR£8m (€10m). Their haul included works by Vermeer, Franz Hals and Goya.

Sir Alfred, who was 71 at the time, and one of his staff were struck with revolvers before being tied up in the library. He was forced to watch as the raiders removed his rare paintings by cutting them from their frames with a screwdriver.

A few days later the director of the National Gallery received a ransom demand for £500,000 (€635,000) as well as the release of the Price sisters, who had been jailed for IRA bombing offences in London.

No ransom was paid and the Gardaí later found the paintings in a cottage and a rented Morris Minor car in Glandore, County Cork. Dugdale was sentenced to nine years in jail, but was released after six.

On 21 May 1986 the house was robbed again – this time by Martin Cahill and his gang. They began by deliberately setting off the security system and retreating to the bushes. The Gardaí came and went, believing it was only a false alarm. An hour later Cahill and his cohorts broke in again and took eighteen paintings, seven of which were found within hours, dumped by the nearby lakes.

However, the 'Mickey Mouse'-boxer-shorts-wearing crook couldn't shift the remaining eleven paintings as they were all too well known. Eventually he did a deal with a loyalist group in the North, who attempted to bring one of the haul (a Metzu miniature) to Turkey to sell on the black market. Instead of meeting interested Turkish art dealers, however, they met some very interested police officers, who were only too glad to relieve them of their little treasure and return it to Ireland.

As of October 2006 two of the original paintings are still missing, believed by many to be hidden in the Dublin Mountains. Others have turned up in Britain and Belgium and, in two cases, behind a sofa in a semi-detached and in an attic.

Sir Alfred passed away in May 1994 at the age of 91, so he didn't have to endure the next two robberies, the penultimate taking place in June 2001 when a Volkswagen Golf was rammed through the front door of his house and a Gainsborough and a Belloto were stolen. The thief responsible is believed to have been one of Cahill's former henchmen, who was looking for a bargaining chip to use in negotiations with the Gardaí over other crimes. They were recovered in September of that year on the southside of Dublin.

Then in September 2003, a Mitsubishi Pajero off-roader with a plank affixed to its rear reversed up the steps and smashed in through a window. Five of the eleven paintings hanging inside, including two Rubens, were nabbed. The entire job, which was caught on

Still it gives a whole new meaning to the phrase 'just nipping out for a quick Beit'.

CCTV, was done in just 50 seconds. However, the thieves could have taken their time as the security guard – who was in his 70s – was in another wing of the house at the time and the nearest police car was in Baltinglass, 26km away.

Still it gives a whole new meaning to the phrase 'just nipping out for a quick Beit'.

INTERESTING FACT

- Massive, spectacular, 100-bedroomed Russborough House was designed by the appropriately named German architect, Richard Castles.

Least Interesting Soccer Manager

This entry should of course read: 'Most Boring Accent etc' but there was an imbalance in the Most/Least ratio when this section was being written. Anyway, here goes: The Least Interesting Soccer Manager is . . . Republic of Ireland manager Steve Staunton. Why? Well, for two reasons.

1. He's from Dundalk
2. The following three words: 'I'm the gaffer.' Put together they sound something like this: 'Kkkhhhaaaimm deugh Gaffaw.'

Listening to a modem starting up for ten minutes through a loud hailer would be soothing compared to having to endure one of Staunton's press conferences. People have been known to get tinnitus of the eyes from reading his newspaper interviews.

Apart from that he's a grand chap.

Most Money Paid For Wigs

One could be forgiven for thinking this money was spent by Ireland's soccer writers after pulling their collective hair out in frustration at trying to understand Steve Staunton in the previous section – but it isn't.

The most money spent on wigs by middle-aged men is €62,318 although, admittedly, a large portion of that was for black gowns as well. The figure is part of a €1.91m expense bill paid to 121 judges for travel, subsistence, judicial attire and incidental expenses in 2005. Of this €996,299 was paid to 49 District Court judges while 33 Circuit Court M'Luds claimed €800,772.

The judicial horse hair wigs referred to here were introduced in 1714 to mark the official mourning of Queen Anne's death. They are also known as 'periwigs' or 'perukes' (but then you probably knew that all ready). A 'merkin', you may be interested to learn, is a pubic wig for women – not that that has anything to do with the judiciary (that we know of)[14].

High Court judges were the biggest spenders in the peruke and gown department and splashed out €31,300 on their court clothing. One even spent €4,566 on his

[14] If you remember anything from this section, it will be the word 'merkin', won't it?

horsehair headgear and incidentals, to be appropriately dressed for his court appearances, unlike one Wicklowman who fell foul of a judge for wearing the ... Least Appropriate Shirt For Court.

Least Appropriate Shirt For Court

A Bray resident was sentenced to seven days in jail for wearing a T-shirt with the words 'Never mind the Bollocks, Here's the Sex Pistols' at the town court in July 2006. The judge refused an attempt by the defendant to purge his 'contempt' after his partner left the court to buy a plain blue T-shirt. The judge said that the defendant hadn't furnished 'good reason' for wearing the offending garment and that his contempt of the court was 'clear and brazen'. The man's partner said he was a life-long Pistols fan and had worn the T-shirt without thinking.

And whatever you think about that judgement, you might spare a thought for how well judged the choice of words was for the following marketing campaigns.

Most Unfortunate Marketing Campaign

Advance warning from the author:
Never, ever, EVER drink and drive. It impairs judgment and makes it harder to get power into your backswing, as any golfer will tell you. As for driving a motor vehicle – don't even consider it, not even if you're a rugby fan.

In February 2006 Guinness' advertising gurus were caught offside when they launched their promotional campaign for the Six Nations championship. The marketing folk appeared to call on rugger fans to drive with a pint of the famed black stuff. Posters which appeared over the 'push' and 'pull' signs on the doors of Dublin's pubs included the rugby exhortations 'drive' and 'heave' – the latter being particularly alarming for punters entering the loo. Red-faced Guinness – who are scrupulously committed to responsible drinking – removed the ambiguous signs after a consumer brought the subliminal message to their attention.

Their gaffe, however, was naught compared to that made by ice cream gurus **Ben and Jerry**. The US food giants, whose mission statement promotes 'deep respect' for individuals, are famous for their imaginatively-named flavours, including: Caramel Chew Chew, Chunky Monkey, Phish Food and Minter Wonderland to name but four. The company, however, found itself offering profuse apologies after it launched a stout-flavoured ice cream called 'Black and Tan'.

In what can best be described as a bit of brain freeze, the affable hippies began promoting their creamy concoction unaware it would evoke memories of the notorious British force that ran amok in Ireland during the War of Independence. In the 1920s, 8,000 of these ex-servicemen arrived in Ireland to keep order as the authorities grappled with attacks by flying columns. Their *modii operandi* were torture, murder and arson – not exactly words that engender a warm, fuzzy feeling inside one's breast.

One can only imagine the calamitous scenes at modern-day street parties in certain parts of the North when someone asks for another scoop of their favourite dessert: 'Well, well, well, Cameron (rubs belly vigorously), I could murder another Black and Tan . . .'

The Vermont-based company said that they had had a small amount of contact from people letting them know how 'Black and Tan' originated and that they hadn't been aware of the connotations. Not that anybody really believed a pair of harmless hippies would be promoting anything other than love and peace in the first place.

Besides, it could have been worse: what if they had decided to extend the range and call it the 'War of Independence Flavour Brigade'? Favourites could have included Carlsberg Special Brugha Flavour, Coca Collins Fizz Bang Surprise or even Padraig Pears and Apples Flavour.

INTERESTING FACT

- Dublin is only the second city in the world to have a Ben and Jerry's Ice Cream flavour named after it. Dublin Mudslide was launched in May 2005, twenty years after New York Super Fudge Chunk first hit the freezers.

Most Pickled Irishman In A Pub

Famed pugilist Dan Donnelly (1788–1820), who is immortalised in a ballad about his boxing match with Englishman George Cooper near Newbridge County Kildare, rested his elbow on a bar for nearly fifty years without respite – morning, noon and night.

Donnelly caught the Irish public's imagination in 1815 when he beat Cooper over 23 brutal minutes for a purse of 60 sovereigns in what is now known as Donnelly's Hollow. Over 20,000 people travelled the 45 km (28 miles) from Dublin to the Hollow to witness the event and Dan became such an heroic figure that he was knighted by King George.

The giant boxer died suddenly in 1820 and grave robbers took his body to the Royal Hospital where a Dr Hall realised who he was and took his right arm as a souvenir, preserving it by dipping it into red-lead paint. The surgeon reburied the rest of the body and brought the arm to a medical college in Scotland. It was later sold on to a circus and became part of a peep show. Over the decades the limb changed hands (if you'll pardon the expression) and in 1949 wound up in the possession of the Byrne family in Kilcullen, County Kildare. They put it on display in a glass case in their pub, The Hideout, for forty-three years. The family sold up in 1995 and Dan's pickled arm is no longer on public display, but kept under lock and key.

Seeing as how the arm was pickled (and legless) during the duration of its stay in the bar, Dan Donnelly's

descendants can proudly claim that he was the Most
Pickled Irishman In A Pub – Ever.

Most Ice Cream Lost At Sea

The greatest dollop of dessert ever lost at sea was 800 kg
of French ice cream aboard the Belfast-built *Titanic*,
which sank on 14 April 1912. The largest ship in the
world was also carrying 40 tonnes of potatoes as well as
5,000 kg of fresh fish, making it, potentially, the largest
floating Fish and Chip shop in the world – if the White
Star Line bothered to capitalise upon that fact.

The greatest amount of dessert ever lost in Irish waters
was '665 packets of confectionarys' recorded in the
manifest of the *Lusitania*, which was torpedoed off the
south coast of Ireland on 7 May 1915. That manifest,
however, has been a source of controversy for the past 90
years and many believe the ship was carrying munitions
when Kapitan-Leutnant Walther Schwieger opened fire
from the submarine, *U20*.

It is now known that the aforementioned 'passenger'
ship was carrying a total of 1,248 cases of Live 3 shrapnel
shells (each case contained four shells) for use by the
Royal Artillery, as well as 90 tonnes of unrefrigerated
butter and cheese destined for the Royal Navy Weapons
Testing Establishment in Essex.

Why the navy 'boffins' wanted such a large quantity of
spoiled dairy products is still a mystery. It's worth noting,
though, that both consignments were insured at the
special government insurance rate and even more curious

is the fact that the insurance was never claimed.

There have been at least fourteen movie / television / Broadway attempts to recount the awful events surrounding the sinking of the *Titanic*. The first was a cobbled together ten-minute newsreel circulated in cinemas immediately after the disaster. Much of the footage is of the older, and more photographed, sister ship, the *Olympic*. Movie-goers of the time were easily taken in by such deceptions.

Possibly the strangest of all *Titanic* 'events' opened on Broadway in 1964. The *Unsinkable Molly Brown* was a musical account of how the real-life Mrs JJ Brown survived the horrors of that night at sea. The film adaptation starred Debbie Reynolds in the title role. 'All Jazz Hands on Deck! All Jazz hands on Deck!' was one of the show's killer numbers – or should have been.

By far the best movie ever made about the *Titanic* was the moving *A Night To Remember* (1958), directed by Roy Baker. Appropriately, the producer responsible for bringing Walter Lord's book to the big screen was an Irishman, William MacQuitty, who had been present at the ship's launch in Belfast in 1911. Remarkably, despite winning a raft of awards, the film did badly at the box office.

The same cannot be said of James Cameron's schmaltzy 1997 offering *Titanic*, which grossed exactly $1,797,374,192 worldwide – this, despite Leonardo Di Caprio's woeful Irish accent and Celine Dion sounding like a demented seagull on the soundtrack. To say it was cheesier than the hold of the *Lusitania* would not be an understatement.

INTERESTING FACTS

- 1,550 lives were lost on the *Titanic* and 1,195 died aboard the *Lusitania*, the latter tragedy being responsible for finally dragging America into the First World War.

- Cameron was not the first filmmaker to use the title *Titanic*. Josef Goebbels got there before him in the 1940s when he commissioned his own celluloid version of events. *Titanic* (1940) (pronounced with a heavy Teutonic accent) was one of the most expensive German movies ever made, although most of the public didn't get to see it, what with the bombing raids and all. Goebbels liked the concept as it showed the British as bunglers.

- The 1980 stinker *Raise The Titanic* cost $40 million and the special effects alone cost more than it took to build the original ship. Unlike the *Titanic* it sank without a trace, prompting movie mogul Lew Grade to groan: 'Raise the Titanic? It would cost less to lower the Atlantic.'

Biggest and Smallest

Biggest *Riverdance*

The first attempt at setting an Irish – not World – *Riverdance* record took place in Vicarstown, County Laois on 30 April 2000. On that day 1,032 people jigged up and down and flailed their legs on the banks of the canal. It was subsequently accepted as the benchmark for all *Riverdance* devotees. However, as it was executed in front of a canal (presumably with a few bicycle wheels and supermarket trollies doubling for an audience) it does not qualify as Biggest Riverdance. On the positive side of things, if producers John McColgan and Moya Doherty as well as composer Bill Whelan and choreographer Michael Flatley decide to sit down and devise a musical called *Canaldance*, the 1,032 'dancers' of Vicarstown would be entitled to special mention in this book. As it stands, they're not.

Which is not the case with the good people of Castlecomer, County Kilkenny...

Biggest Wellie Race

For the past thirty years Castlecomer has held the World's Only St Stephen's Day Wellington Boot Race. The course covers 6.5 km and has an average turnout of more than 400 runners, (each wearing wellies naturally enough).

There is growing speculation that the introduction of wellies into the race is more recent than the Castlecomerians would have the world believe. The run was first conceived in 1975 as an excuse to get the townspeople out in the air after the Christmas Day celebrations. As there had been nothing on RTÉ on Christmas night except for re-runs of *Mannix*, interspersed with the adventures of Czech cartoon characters, Lolek and Bolek, a large number of people had got themselves very drunk and so turned out the following morning to clear their heads. The spectacle was such a success that it became an annual – and very orthodox – event.

This was to change on 26 December 1995 when holiday-maker and prominent Gaeilgeoir, **Jasper Ó Críotháin** fell into the River Dinin. Apparently, Ó Críotháin had become obsessed with *Riverdance* after witnessing it during the Eurovision the previous May. Like the native Castlecomerians, he had decided to get blind drunk on Christmas night rather than watch RTÉ and was still in a state of considerable inebriation the following morning when he tried some riverdancing of his own. Unlike Michael Flatley, who has the ability to walk on water, Jasper sank with a loud splash after jumping off the bridge into the icy river. It took sixty locals in wellies and waders five minutes to drag him out and subsequently chase him out of town while administering their boots to his sodden backside. This is where the tradition of racing in wellies began – or maybe not.

INTERESTING FACTS

- *Riverdance*, which was initially a seven-minute interval during the 1994 Eurovision at The Point in Dublin (and was watched by 300 million viewers), has since played to 19 million people worldwide and sold 10 million DVDs/videos to date.
- The number of people who have never seen *Riverdance* is greater than the number of those who have – which is consoling.
- Michael Flatley's hairspray is the same stuff they use to hold the wings on old-fashioned airplanes.

Smallest Paddy's Day Parade

This took place in Dalkey, County Dublin in 1996. It was under 2 m long and went out one door of Dan Finnegan's Public House and in the other in a record time of 5 sec. It was raining and we both needed to pee.

Smallest Person With A Big Brain

Schoolboy Domhnall Ryan from Knocklyon, County Dublin managed to teach his contemporaries a thing or thirty-two when he won the BBC's *Junior Mastermind* title in front of a television audience of millions in February 2006. The competition, which is based on the classic quiz for adults, pits ten- and eleven-year-olds from Britain and Ireland against each other, as they sit in the famous black leather chair. One at a time, that is. Not all together at once – although, being small, some of them might fit in the chair at the same time. That would be just silly though and they'd all be trying to talk over each other and then the pinching and general schoolboy messing would begin.

Where were we? Domhnall has a mighty head on his shoulders and made it through the televised heats and into the last six with ease. His specialist subject in the final was 'Mammals of the African Plains' on which he scored 17 points. At the half-way mark he was in joint second and then scored 14 in the 'General Knowledge' round leaving him tied with another contestant. Bearing up brilliantly under pressure, Domhnall won the subsequent play-off and became the first Irish boy to win the title. Remarkably he wasn't the only person from this island to win *Mastermind* with 31 points. The other person also happened to be the world's . . . Biggest *Father Ted* Fan.

Biggest *Father Ted* Fan

Patrick Gibson is unparalleled in his game show achievements on these islands. Not only did he bank the staggering stg£1m jackpot on ITV's *Who Wants to be a Millionaire* in 2004 but he also won the 28th *Mastermind* crown in 2005. The software developer dad of two beat a university lecturer and a freelance translator to score the aforementioned 31 points with no passes and so took the famous crystal bowl home.

Wigan-based Patrick, who went to university in Belfast, dazzled John Humphrys and the studio audience with his amazing store of knowledge. However, it was for his inspired choice of specialist subject that he will forever be remembered – the cult Channel 4 comedy *Father Ted*.

Patrick scored 17 points out of 18 questions making him the Biggest *Father Ted* Fan in history. The only question he got wrong was the unlucky 13th, which was: 'In the episode 'Hell', Mrs Doyle said she had put cocaine in the cake but then realised she meant what?' Patrick's answer was: 'Cinnamon.' The correct answer was: 'Raisins.'

The quiz brainiac, by the by, was born in Galway, which is home to the Shortest River in Ireland, the **Corrib**. The Corrib, at 6.4 km long, is only 1/56th of the length of Ireland's Longest River, which is the **Shannon**. And that, by a remarkable coincidence, is where we started (*see* Page 1).